THE FUNDAMENTALS OF FILM-MAKING

An AVA Book

—

Published by AVA Publishing SA

Rue des Fontenailles 16
Case Postale
1000 Lausanne 6
Switzerland

Tel: +41 786 005 109
Email: enquiries@avabooks.ch

—

Distributed by Thames & Hudson
(ex-North America)

181a High Holborn
London WC1V 7QX
United Kingdom

Tel: +44 20 7845 5000
Fax: +44 20 7845 5055
Email: sales@thameshudson.co.uk
www.thamesandhudson.com

Distributed in the USA & Canada by:
Watson-Guptill Publications
770 Broadway
New York, New York 10003
USA

Fax: +1 646 654 5487
Email: info@watsonguptill.com
www.watsonguptill.com

—

English Language Support Office
AVA Publishing (UK) Ltd.

Tel: +44 1903 204 455
Email: enquiries@avabooks.co.uk

ISBN 2-940373-19-1 & 978-2-940373-19-2

10 9 8 7 6 5 4 3 2 1

Design by Mr Smith's Letterpress Workshop

Cover images copyright Getty Images
Production by AVA Book
Production Pte. Ltd., Singapore

Tel: +65 6334 8173
Fax: +65 6259 9830
Email: production@avabooks.com.sg

—

All reasonable attempts have been made to trace, clear and credit the copyright holders of the images reproduced in this book. However, if any credits have been inadvertently omitted, the publisher will endeavour to incorporate amendments in future editions.

THE FUNDAMENTALS OF FILM-MAKING

JANE BARNWELL

THE FUNDAMENTALS OF FILM-MAKING

Table of Contents

The Fundamentals of Film-Making is intended to provide an overview of the film-making process for those people who work, study and have an interest in film. Through detailed explanation and the use of film stills, illustrations and diagrams, this book offers a unique resource to the practical and collaborative process of making a film.

1: CHAPTER INTRODUCTIONS
Provide a brief outline of the key concepts and ideas that the chapter will explore.

2: CAPTIONS
Supply information about the images and help connect the visuals with the key concepts discussed in the body copy.

HOW TO GET THE MOST OUT OF THIS BOOK

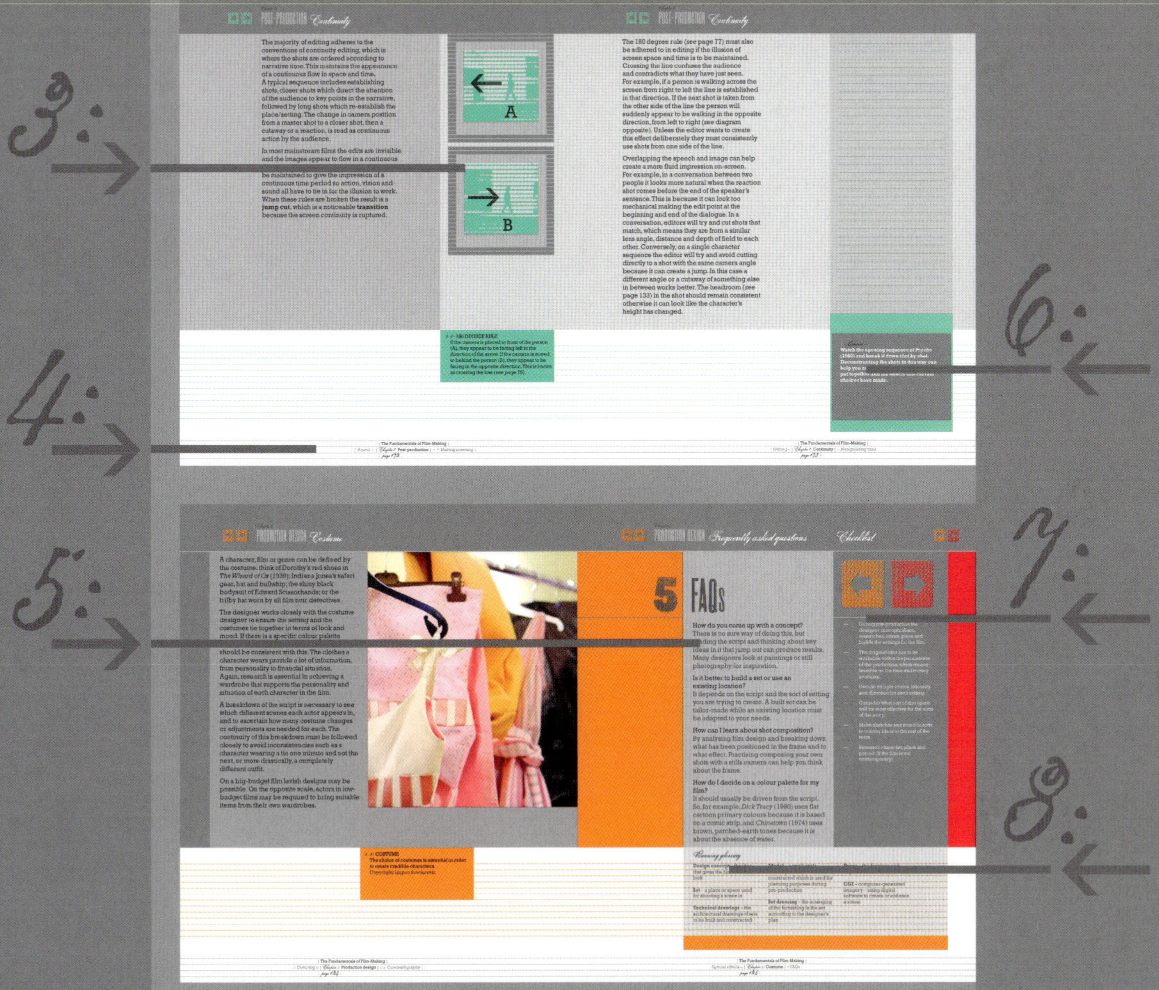

3:

4:

5:

6:

7:

8:

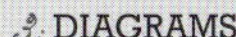

3: **DIAGRAMS**
Help to explain technical concepts in more detail.

4: **NAVIGATION**
Helps you determine which chapter unit you are in and what the preceding and following sections are.

5: **FAQs**
A useful reference providing quick answers to the most frequently asked questions.

6: **EXERCISES**
Appear throughout the chapters to help reinforce the topic being explored.

7: **CHECKLIST**
Provides a summary of the essential elements that should be considered for each of the stages involved in creating a film.

8: **GLOSSARY**
Provided at the end of each chapter to define and explain the initial use of technical terms or phrases.

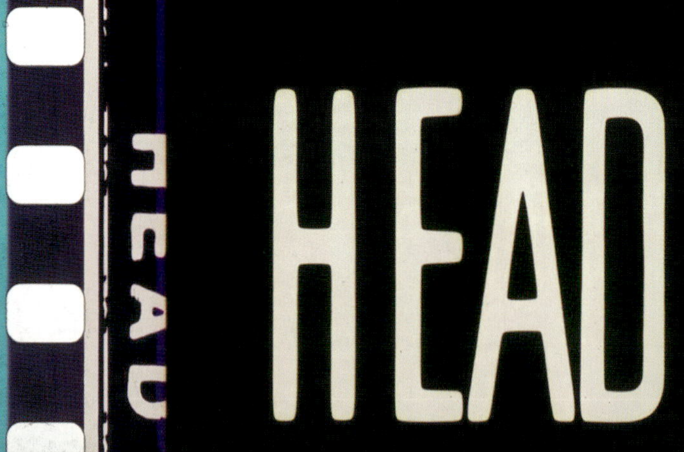
PICTURE
HEAD

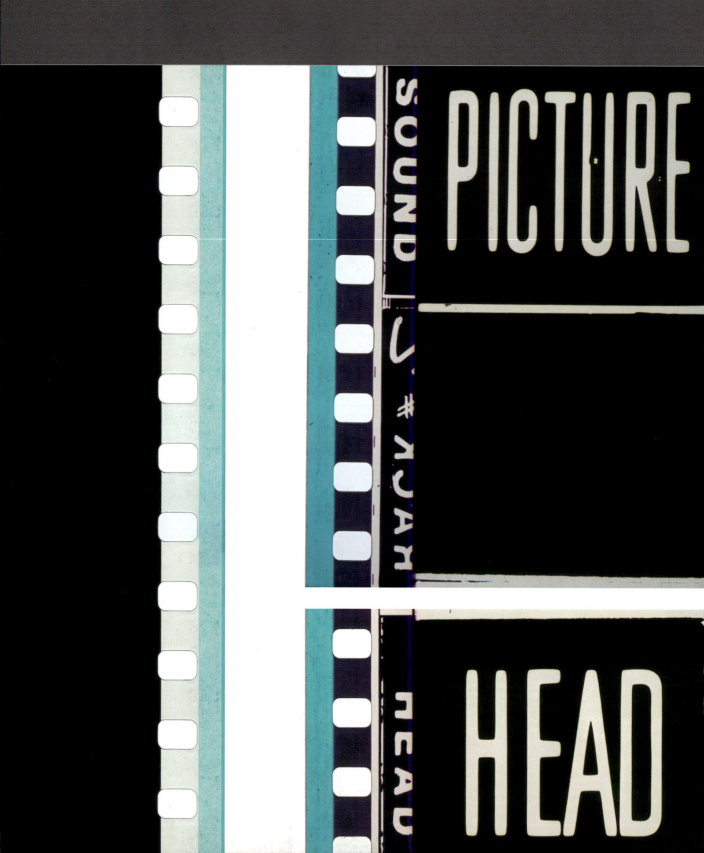

INTRODUCTION

When a film is shot on-location a crowd of interested onlookers soon forms. What is it they are drawn to? What are they hoping to see? A glimpse of a big star? Perhaps it is something more intangible – watching all the elements coming together to create the screen image; the point at which the lighting, equipment, cast and crew all come together to record a carefully constructed fragment in time. This book may be like that moment – when you see everything come together and begin to get a sense of what is actually involved in film-making.

Film is a huge part of our everyday lives. Not only do we spend time consuming and discussing film, it also infiltrates our consciousness and carves out ideas about the world and its inhabitants. The impact of and fascination with film is such that a great deal has been written in the area of both film theory and practice. This book looks to provide an overview of the film-making process mapping out the practical, technical and creative aspects involved, exploring how each decision made impacts on the end product.

From the opening sequence of a film we enter into the world constructed by the makers. Choices of place and time immediately supply context. The actors, the music, titles and pace of editing suggest the way the story may unfold over the next couple of hours. Different types of shot are selected and combined in such a way as to provide information about where and when the film is set, who the key characters are and why they are there. The imagination and organisation required to make a film is reflected in the stunning diversity of films produced today. The practical process remains fundamentally the same, scaling up or down in relation to the size of the available budget.

Technology is ever changing in our technically-driven lives, and film technology is no exception – from the format used to shoot on to the way in which it is consumed. Film as a medium is always evolving and with each big change comes concern for the future popularity of the medium. The audience, however, continually adapts, often welcoming the changes as film reaches different stages of maturity. Technology is not dealt with in this book in terms of details of advances in shooting and editing equipment. The focus instead is on the fundamentals that remain in spite of changing technology; if you can appreciate how to compose a shot effectively it will translate across all formats and all technologies.

The visual material provided throughout the book aims to illustrate aspects of film-making and to bring to life ideas explained within the text. A range of images has been used, from students and young film-makers to people at the top of their profession. The intention is to make the process accessible and encourage enthusiasts at every stage of learning. What this book should not do is mystify film-making as something implausibly difficult, shrouded in inaccessible language.

Film-making progresses through three stages: pre-production, production and post-production. This book reflects these processes by having chapters that are divided into each of the major departments: Script, Production, Direction, Production Design, Cinematography, Sound and Post-Production. The book opens with an introduction to the film crew and the closing chapter considers ways of analysing and theorising film, providing context and making connections between film theory and practice.

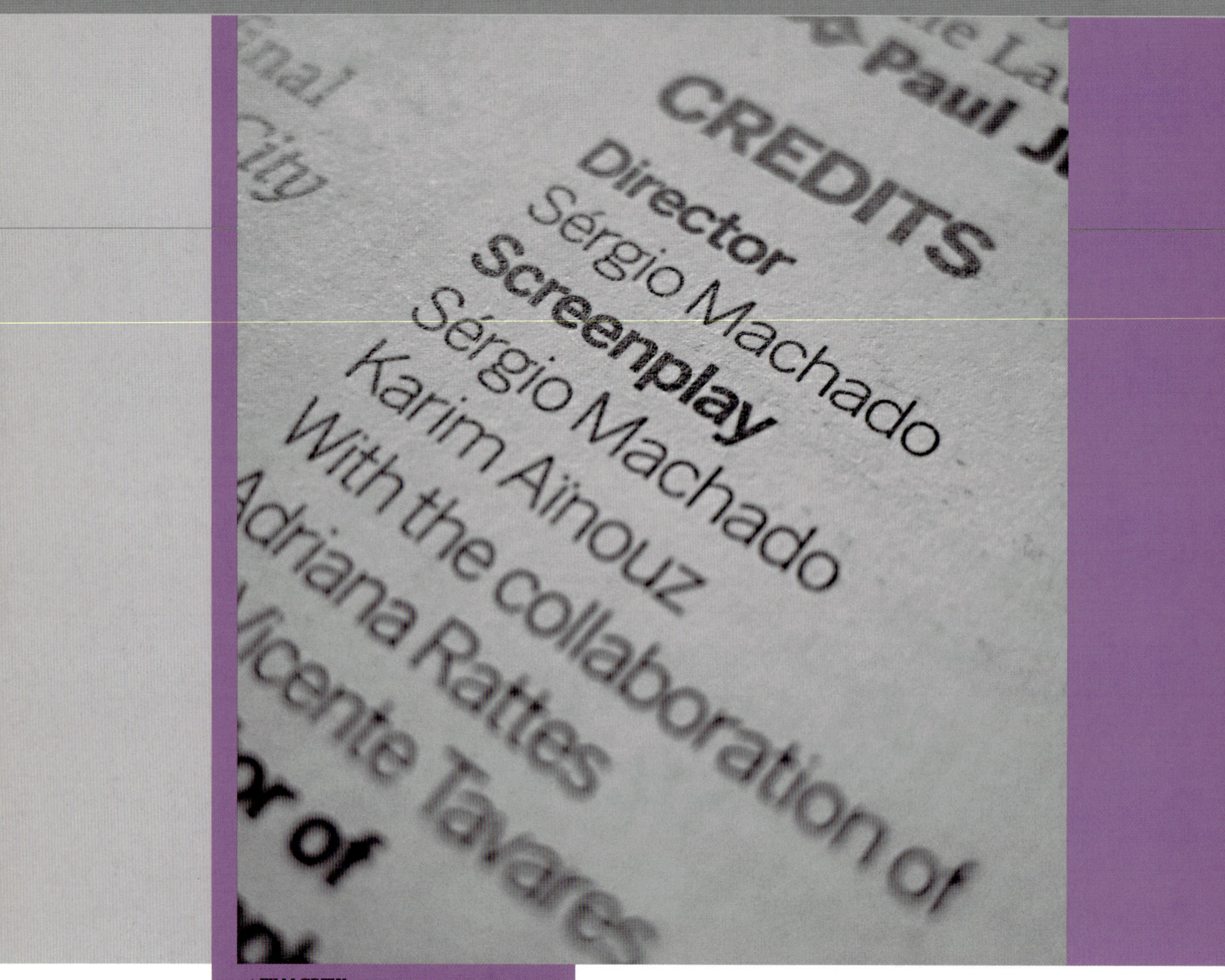

1: FILM CREW
There are a vast number of personnel involved in making a film, and each has an important role to play – both individually and as part of the team.

1 THE TEAM

The vast array of credits at the end of a film can be confusing for the uninitiated. This section will unravel and explain some of the key roles, indicating how the team or crew collaborate to produce the finished film.

Employment is usually on a freelance basis, which means each job is project-based and does not lead to a sustained term of employment. Having said this, word of mouth plays a big part and crew often recommend each other for their next project.

The size of the crew will increase or decrease in line with the film budget and genre. A small drama crew for a student production may comprise of just the heads of each department while a documentary may be created by a single person. This section provides an overview of the departments and some of the roles within them.

THE TEAM

SCRIPTWRITING → PRODUCING → DIRECTING →

POST-PRODUCTION

Departments and job descriptions

The crew is divided into departments, each specialising in a particular aspect of the production. Different departments come on-board at different stages in the production and all work within the limitations of schedule and budget.

Films are very rarely shot in narrative sequence. A shooting schedule is drawn up where shooting days are organised around locations and actor availability rather than narrative continuity, which saves time and money.

When the lines of communication operate effectively the smooth running of the production is achieved. If problems occur the entire system can break down, which will impact on the finished film. Each person on the film should know what they are responsible for and to whom they report.

There are various routes into the film industry profession and crew members come from many different backgrounds. Runners or assistants starting in each department may work their way up in an apprentice fashion, learning from experts. However, crew are just as likely to have come from film school, college courses, work experience or vocational schemes, such as Skillset in the UK.

SCRIPT
Writers are responsible for the raw material of the screenplay. They develop the idea into an outline treatment and then a script. There may be more than one writer working on a project. The writer's involvement can end when the script goes into production or may continue in an advisory role.

PRODUCTION
A **Producer** initiates, coordinates, supervises and controls the logistics, such as funding, hiring crew and distribution. The producer is involved throughout the film-making process from development to completion. Their first task is to find money in order to develop the idea into a script or to buy an existing script. Funding may come from private or public sector sources. A budget is constructed based on available funding, which may result in changes, such as fewer filming days or locations to keep costs down. Each department is allocated a budget to work within.

The **Production Manager** supervises the physical aspects of the production including personnel, technology, budget and scheduling. It is the production manager's responsibility to make sure that filming stays on schedule and within budget.

The **Location Manager** researches, locates, secures and coordinates the filming locations by identifying the precise locations needed. The Location Manager works closely with the Director and the Production Designer.

The **Unit Manager** fulfils the same role as the Production Manager, but for secondary-unit shooting. There may be several units depending on the scale of production.

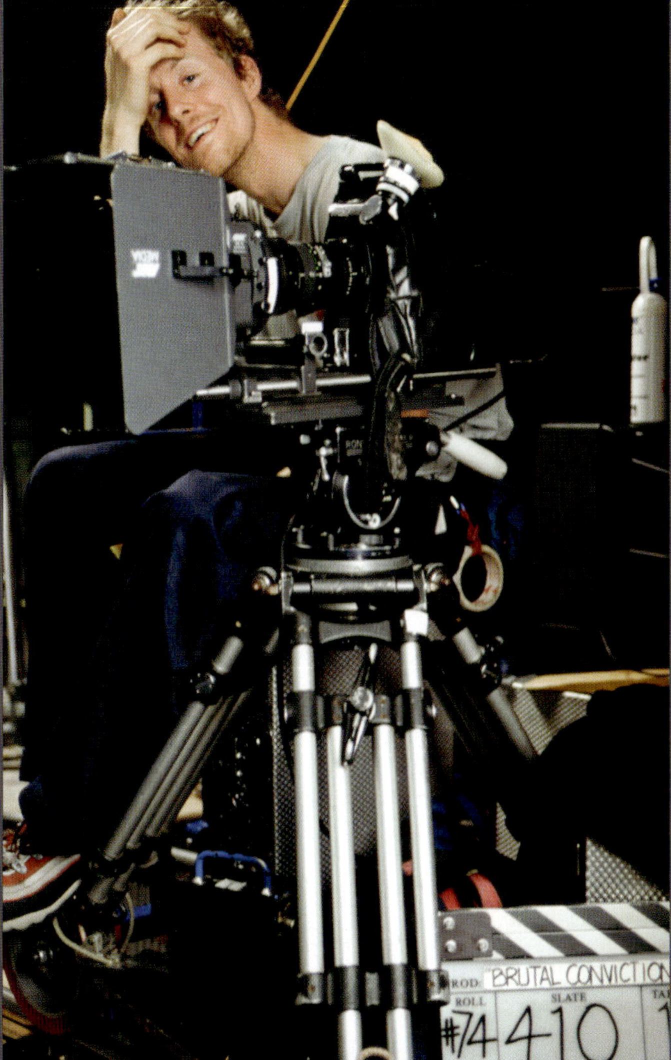

1: CAMERA CREW
The camera crew are vital in ensuring the effective cinematography of the film.

2: THE DIRECTOR
The Director is responsible for the overall approach to the film and works closely with the First Assistant Director (1st AD) to ensure that all aspects of the shoot run smoothly.

DIRECTION

The Direction Department is headed up by the Director but also includes many lesser-known roles within the team.

The **Director** is responsible for the vision and overall approach to a film, overseeing the creative aspects, including directing the actors and the camera. The Director storyboards certain scenes in order to plan how they will be shot in detail. They decide how actors should move and deliver their lines in each scene.

The **First Assistant Director (1st AD)** takes care of logistics on the set and manages each take. This is more of a practical than a creative role that provides assistance to the Production Manager and Director. The aim of the 1st AD is to ensure that filming stays on schedule and to maintain a productive working environment. The 1st AD is in charge of overseeing the day-to-day management of the cast and crew, scheduling, equipment, script and set.

The **Second Assistant Director (2nd AD)** assists the 1st AD and liaises with the cast. They may also direct background action. There are 3rd ADs in the Canadian and British crew structures, but the American system tends to have 2nd 2nd ADs.

The **Script Supervisor** ensures that what is shot maintains continuity of action, dialogue and vision, so that in spite of being shot out of sequence the edit will be in the chronological order of the script. They keep track of what parts of the script are shot and make notes on each take, thereby ensuring that consistency is maintained from shot to shot. The Script Supervisor works very closely with the Director on-set.

1: DIRECTION
The Director is responsible for the actors and for how they perform in front of the camera.

ART DEPARTMENT

The Art Department creates the physical world of the film. This is essential because the environment the characters inhabit helps to convey ideas in the script and transports the audience into cinematic space. Choices will be made about using real locations and studio sound stages, and often a combination of the two will be utilised. On a big picture there may be several sets built at once. The Art Department is often the largest department on a film.

The **Production Designer (PD)** is the head of the Art Department and produces the visual identity of the film, thus creating the physical appearance – settings and properties. The Production Designer is brought in early in pre-production and is responsible for drawing, construction, dressing, shooting and then striking (taking down and disposing) of the set. The Production Designer works closely with the Director and the Cinematographer to achieve a coherent look.

The **Art Director** works for the PD and oversees craftspeople, such as the Set Designer and Set Decorator, who carry out the production design.

The **Set Designer (draftsman)**, often an architect, drafts the structures or interior spaces called for by the Production Designer.

The **Standby Art Director** monitors the set during filming ensuring the PD's designs remain as intended during shooting.

The **Set Decorator** works closely with the Production Designer and the Art Director. They are in charge of the decorating, including the furnishings and all the other objects that will be seen in the film.

The **Buyer** locates and then purchases or rents the set dressing in conjunction with the Set Decorator.

The **Set Dressers** physically dress the set with furniture, drapes, carpet etc.

The **Supervising Art Director** manages the Art Department budget and schedule.

The **Property Master (Props Master)** is in charge of finding and managing all the props that appear in the film.

Props Builders construct the props that are used for the film (plaster casting, machining and electronics).

The **Armourer** is a specialised props technician who deals with firearms.

The **Construction Coordinator** oversees the construction of all the sets. The coordinator orders materials, schedules the work, and supervises the crew of carpenters and painters.

The **Scenic Artist** is responsible for the surface treatments of the sets. This includes special paint effects, such as aging and gilding, as well as simulating the appearance of wood, stone, brick, metal and so forth.

COSTUME

The Costume Department is responsible for the design, fitting, hire, purchase and care of all wardrobe items.

The **Costume Designer** provides all the costumes worn by the actors. They design the garments including the fabric, colours and sizes. They work closely with the Director to interpret character and the Production Designer to achieve a coherent approach.

The **Costume Supervisor** manages the wardrobe and helps translate the designer's ideas into reality. They make decisions on the sourcing of items, the hiring and firing of support staff, the budget, paperwork and department logistics.

The **Costume Standby** is present on-set at all times, monitoring the quality and continuity of the costumes before and during takes.

The **Wardrobe Supervisor** is in charge of the running of the wardrobe once shooting starts.

HAIR AND MAKE-UP

Make-up artists design and apply make-up to the cast. Their role is to adjust the actors' appearance to suit the role and character to be played.

The **Hair Stylist** works in conjunction with the make-up artist and is responsible for maintaining and styling the hair of anyone appearing on-screen.

SPECIAL EFFECTS DEPARTMENT

The Special Effects Department is responsible for creating the physical effects in the film, including atmospherics such as rain or snow. Computer-Generated Images (CGI), such as dramatic tidal waves or destructive bombs, are also managed by this department.

^ *1:* THE ART DEPARTMENT
The Art and Costume Departments are responsible for creating the physical world of the film.

CAMERA AND LIGHT DEPARTMENT

Shot composition, movement and light all combine to create the cinematography of a film. The camera crew are the operators of the equipment that make this a reality.

The **Cinematographer or Director of Photography (DOP)** is the head of the camera and lighting department. They make decisions on lighting and framing in conjunction with the Director, translating the Director's vision through technical choices like aperture, filter and lighting.

The Camera Operator uses the camera at the direction of the Cinematographer or the Director. Generally, a Cinematographer doesn't operate the camera, but sometimes these jobs may be combined.

The **First Assistant Camera (1st AC)** is responsible for focusing and refocusing the camera lens during shooting.

The **Second Assistant Camera (2nd AC)** assists in positioning and moving the camera. The 2nd AC oversees the notes and records when the film stock is received, used, and sent to the lab for processing. Additionally, the 2nd AC organises the camera equipment and its transport from one location to another.

The **Clapper Loader** operates the clapperboard at the beginning of each take and loads the film stock into the camera magazines between takes. It is the responsibility of the loader to manage the inventory of film and communicate with the 1st AC regarding film usage and the remaining stock throughout the day. With digital photography, this position is often eliminated.

Grips are the lighting and rigging technicians who build and operate the equipment that supports the camera, tripods, dollies, tracks, jibs and cranes. They work closely with the electrical department to assemble the lighting set-ups required for a shot.

The **Video Assist Operator** is in charge of video playback to enable the team to monitor what is being shot.

« 1: CAMERA AND LIGHTING
Shot composition and lighting are carefully combined to create the cinematography of the film. Each are vital in order to create the desired effects.

LIGHTING
The **Gaffer (Chief Lighting Technician)** is the head of the electrical department, and is responsible for the design and execution of the lighting plan.

The **Best Boy Electric** is the chief assistant to the Gaffer.

Lighting Technicians (Sparks) set-up and control lighting equipment.

SOUND
The **Sound Mixer** is the head of the Sound Department on-set, and is responsible for recording all sound during filming. This involves the selection and combination of microphones, operation of a sound-recording device and, sometimes, the mixing of audio signals in real time.

The **Boom Operator** is an assistant to the Sound Mixer, and is responsible for microphone placement and movement during filming. The Boom Operator uses a boom pole – a long piece of equipment that allows precise positioning of the microphone above or below the actors out of the camera frame.

EDITING AND POST-PRODUCTION
The **Film Editor** assembles the various shots into a coherent film, with the help of the Director. The Editor can reinterpret the film through transitions, juxtaposition and pace.

The **Colourist** adjusts the colour of the film for greater consistency or artistic effect using a photochemical process. Digital tools can also be used to manipulate the image, which allows greater creative freedom.

The **Negative Cutter** cuts and splices the negatives as directed by the Editor, and then provides the assembled negative reels to the lab in order for prints to be made.

The **Visual Effects Supervisor** is in charge of the visual effects, where alterations to the film's images are made in post-production. Visual effects should not to be confused with special effects, which are done during production (on-set).

A **Compositor** is a visual-effects artist who composites images from different sources such as video, film, computer-generated 3-D imagery, 2-D animations, paintings, photographs and text.

The **Sound Designer** is in charge of the post-production sound. This role can be highly creative in some instances and at other times it may involve the more straightforward task of working with the Director and Editor to balance the sound.

The **Dialogue Editor** assembles and edits all the dialogue in the soundtrack.

The **Sound Editor** is responsible for assembling and editing all the sound effects in the soundtrack.

The **Music Supervisor** works with the Composer, Mixers and Editors to create the music. They liaise with the film production and the music industry to negotiate the rights for all music tracks used.

The **Composer** writes the musical score for a film.

The **Foley Artist** is the person who creates and records many of the sound effects for the soundtrack.

Post-production on a feature may take up to ten weeks. When all of the editing is finished the film is ready for distribution. Some films secure distribution deals beforehand, others take the finished film to markets such as Cannes and try to secure deals there.

Transport and Catering should not be forgotten as they are two departments that are essential to the success of the film.

1: GRIPS
The Camera Grips are responsible for building and operating the cameras and supporting equipment.

2: THE DIRECTOR OF PHOTOGRAPHY
The Director of Photography (DOP) translates the Director's vision of the film into technical choices.

Collaborating and working as a team

When creating a film it is essential that all departments work closely with one another. At the same time, it is vital to have an understanding of each of the department's functions and responsibilities. Students often want to ignore these roles and work together on everything, which generally ends in tears. Problems tend to arise around confusion over who is responsible for what aspect of the film. It can also be very time-consuming to debate every decision with the entire team and can result in an overly democratic product that is lacking clear direction.

Communication is at the heart of the enterprise – it is the essential key to a strong team. Having an overview of what the different departments do helps communication, leads to an effective working environment and, ultimately, creates a stronger film.

Each of the departments involved in working on a film bring creative, artistic, technical, administrative and interpersonal skills, all of which are essential in the successful running of a set and the making of a film. It is the Producer's responsibility to select and hire the right people for the job – team members who are dedicated to working together during the long and unsociable hours of filming.

1: WORKING AS A TEAM
The hard work of the team all comes together during the actual shooting of the film.

FAQs

How do I find out which department I should work in?
Contact film and TV companies and try to arrange a visit or work experience to learn more about the different jobs. Talk to people and find out if their job is in practice the way you imagine it to be.

Where can I learn more?
There are lots of short courses where you can get a taste of different aspects of film-making.

Look online at sites, such as Shooting People (shootingpeople.org), that advertise for film crew (often unpaid) to gain experience and meet others with similar aims. (*See* Appendix for online education resources.)

How can I get a job in film-making?
Make your own short films and build up a showreel of work. Build contacts and experience in the film industry.

How can I get experience?
Contact film production companies and ask for work experience and keep making your own films.

—
Producing requires strong negotiating skills – shop around and get the best prices available.

—
Costs can be kept down by limiting the number of locations and the distance between them.

—
Shooting on a digital format rather than film will be cost effective.

—
Keeping crew size to a minimum will also save money.

—
Using available light where possible will cut down on the cost of lighting hire.

His 'n Hers

A short film script by Campbell Graham.

FADE IN:

INT. HIS 'N HERS BEDROOM. DAY.

Morning sun streams through onto a couple's discarded clothes.... a bedside book "When I say No I Feel Guilty." In bed, HE, a twenty-something bloke, rolls over to HER, a similarly-aged woman, and fondles her right breast gently from behind through her T-shirt.

Her eyes open but he doesn't see. She shifts his hand away from her breast to hold it by her stomach. His eyes are open – disappointed. After a moment she gets out of bed and shuffles from the room.

INT. KITCHEN. DAY

The couple eat egg and beans in silence at the table. She wolfs her beans down voraciously. He looks down, discontented, and stabs his egg yolk with a knife.

She notices him but then cuts round her yolk, forks it into her mouth whole and bites down in ecstasy. He looks down bitterly and starts corralling his egg yolk with a knife. The clink on the plate takes up a rhythm...

DISSOLVE TO:

EXT. STREET. DAY.

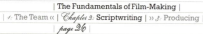

1: HIS 'N HERS SCRIPT PAGE
The layout of the script pages enable easy recognition and effective communication between cast and crew.
Writer/director: Campbell Graham

2 SCRIPTWRITING

How do you conjure an idea for a film? What inspires you to sit down and start writing? The creative urge can come from many places; life, friends, the news, a photograph, a painting, dreams or a piece of music are all classic starting points. Try tapping into hopes and fears – your most embarrassingly cringeworthy moment or deepest desires are often where you will find the best material. Keep an ideas notebook, adding to it whenever you see or hear something that sparks your imagination.

Individuality is the key to making the script special and it is that fresh and original interpretation that will make the work stand out. What is it you want to say? Whether the aim is to educate, inform or entertain, a film can be a powerful tool.

Treatments

When you have an idea the next step is to write a **treatment** (also known as a **synopsis**), which summarises the key events in the story. There is much debate about the best way to format a treatment and it is often unclear what should be included in this paperwork. Here are some guidelines to help navigate the journey.

The treatment outlines the major events in the plot, in the present tense, without using dialogue. It should concisely convey a clear sense of the story, who the characters are and what they want. Names are written in capitals to help with quick identification. The length varies from two pages for a short film to between five and twelve pages for a feature film.

When writing a treatment start with the premise, which is three or four lines detailing the who, what, when and where of the story. The premise should capture the core of the script, succinctly describing what the story is about, and is often a question followed by a complication. The premise should be intriguing and original. Once the premise is established, the next stage is to write the body of the treatment, where the key story events are summarised.

The point of writing a treatment is to help clarify ideas; by committing them to paper you can begin to see what is effective and what isn't. A treatment is also often used as a sales tool, to be sent to potential producers to generate interest in the making of the film. Therefore, it needs to be as quick and easy to digest as possible. In a few short pages the reader should get a strong sense of the concept, story and characters. It is a condensed version of the film you intend to make and should emphasise all the strong points to help convince others it is worth producing.

It can be helpful to produce a scene outline next, where the skeleton of each scene is written up on an index card. Each card should include the key story events of that scene and the characters involved. The order of scenes can be easily manipulated by moving the cards into various sequences, depending on how you want to tell the story. The cards can be rearranged until you are satisfied with the structure.

The next stage is writing the screenplay, which includes what happens (the action) and what is said (the dialogue), but does not include camera directions, which are added later by the director (*see* Chapter 4).

His 'n Hers

(Synopsis for a 10-minute film.)

His 'n Hers is a comedy with a slightly raw centre in which a young couple have an escalating argument about how often they have sex.

1. HIM and HER are having a Sunday lie-in. The sun streams across the bed. He awakes behind her, and starts to fondle her. Her eyes open, she takes his hand away then escapes gently from the bed.

2. They eat their egg and beans in silence. SHE shovels her beans down voraciously, HE watches, then stabs his egg yolk. She cuts around her egg yolk then puts it whole into her mouth and bites. In ecstasy she is unaware of him looking at her but then senses his gaze. He starts to corral his yolk with a knife.

3. They walk down a street to the rhythm of the knife. SHE complains about the pressure he puts on her for sex. HE denies this and claims it's survival of the species. She reminds him that he doesn't want babies. A buxom young woman approaches them. They both notice her. SHE checks to see if he's gawping. He turns quickly to look at a shop window then looks back at her smiling innocently.

4. At a bus-stop, she claims there's always a lump nudging her in bed so feels she can never do anything to get him going. They bicker about whether if he didn't initiate things anything would ever happen.

5. At the park SHE flies her kite – bright colours against the blue sky. She stands serenely looking up at it. HE enters the frame three times with increasingly ridiculous arguments about why they should "do it" (the "sexual receptivity theory" the "blueballs" problem and the "stone age dominant male angle") and she fends him off wittily each time. Only her kite quivering in the breeze gives us a clue to her rising irritation.

(His 'n Hers, synopsis, Page 2)

6. At another bus-stop SHE tries to turn the tables and politely asks a woman beside them if she could tell them how often she and her partner have sex. She claims an impressive 6 or 7 times a week after 4 years. HE is encouraged by this and asks the same of a worldly looking bloke beside him. He says he and his other half kiss and cuddle a lot but to be honest only do it once every six weeks or so. SHE is heartened, but the woman beside her suddenly asks her how often they do it. C.U. of HER looking very uncomfortable.

7. Back in their bedroom that evening – C.U. of HER exploding into rage at his constant harassment. There follows a longer roving scene where the real interplay of power and need comes to the surface – SHE claims his technique has become boring, HE claims she lies there like a wet fish, SHE tells him if he doesn't like it to xxxx off – he doesn't want to – HIS friend Kathy with the big tits is brought into the conversation, the "baby" question is explored further, and there is discussion of his "smelly breath".

... A slight lull where neither of them can go on, she says she's going to stay at "Sal's" – she says it's not working, he (becoming more vulnerable) claims it is working and that there's more to their relationship than just sex. She grabs a bag, and her toothbrush from the bathroom and walks out the door, he pleads with her tearfully to stay, wearing his boxer shorts, runs in for his trousers, realises he hasn't enough time, then to the window in floods claiming he was so lonely before he met her, she says he shouldn't just be a cure for his loneliness, he breaks down, she comes back inside to comfort him, she kisses the tears away and they disappear downwards out of frame. We are left with a twinkling vista of the city at night.

1 – 2: SAMPLE TREATMENT/SYNOPSIS
This treatment (also known as a synopsis) uses standard layout conventions, making it easily accessible to all those who need to use it.

Screenplay – format and layout

1 EXT. THE FOREST – DUSK

The echo of distant cries. We

Past leaves and branches…towar

2 INT. DINING ROOM – HOUSE – NI

A radio issues a tense report…

RADIO REPORTER
. . . now believed to be
three murders. And in a
this morning, D.I. Harr
anyone living within a
the forest to be especia
making sure that they cl
and lock all . . .

CLARA RANDALL switches the rad

3. INT. HALLWAY – HOUSE – NIGHT

The young woman makes her way to

Slowly she turns and stares at th

Hesitantly, Clara walks towards i

There is a noise from behind. Sh

But the hall is empty. She stares

Brutal Conviction – 1.

1 EXT. THE FOREST – DUSK

The echo of distant cries. We glide through the woods…

Past leaves and branches…towards a house… and an open window.

2 INT. DINING ROOM – HOUSE – NIGHT

A radio issues a tense report…

RADIO REPORTER
. . . now believed to be responsible for all
three murders. And in a police statement
this morning, D.I. Harriet Rawlings warned
anyone living within a two mile radius of
the forest to be especially vigilant . . .
making sure that they close all windows
and lock all . . .

CLARA RANDALL switches the radio off and closes the window.

3 INT. HALLWAY – HOUSE – NIGHT

The young woman makes her way to the kitchen. But stops half-way

Slowly she turns and stares at the front door…it is slightly aja

Hesitantly, Clara walks towards it when…

There is a noise from behind. She spins round fast…

But the hall is empty. She stares into the kitchen…

4 INT. KITCHEN – HOUSE

Close on a couple of eggs reaching the boil.

5 INT. HALLWAY – HOUSE

She turns back. Opens the door and looks out…

6 INT/EXT. HOUSE/THE FOREST – NIGHT

Leaves rustle and the white sheets on the washing line blow wild

She listens to the howling wind…it must have forced the door ope

7 INT. HALLWAY – HOUSE – NIGHT

Slamming the door shut she hears a creaking noise from upstairs.

She looks up at the stairs…

Nothing is there. She doesn't move for a moment. She can't.

She tuts…this is ridiculous. So she creeps towards the stairs.

BAMMMMM!…a MASKED FIGURE smashes her against the wall. She gasps

He raises a sharp knife and thrusts it down. She screams out lou

We move over the blood stained walls… over bloody palm-prints…

8 INT/EXT. HOUSE/THE FOREST – NIGHT

Through the open the door the white sheets are now tinged with
blood.

A TV presenter pulls back the sheets abruptly…

1–2: SCRIPT WRITING CONVENTIONS
Each scene is individually numbered.
Each scene starts with EXT (exterior) or INT (interior).
The location is provided.
The time of day (DAY/NIGHT) is specified.

Screenplay – format and layout

The screenplay is a written description of the film, which includes setting, dialogue, character descriptions and actions. It is a map for the film-maker to follow, a means to an end, rather than a product in itself.

All scripts are divided into scenes, which are sections of continuous action set in a single location, changing when there is either a different time, location or both. Each new scene begins with a heading, which includes information about place and time.

The layout is designed to enable easy recognition and effective communication between cast and crew. The script contains only that which can be captured on film and, as such, it is perpetually in the present. Even when there are flashbacks they are portrayed through the context of the present tense. The script should allow the reader to watch the film unfold in their mind as it would on-screen. You should try and 'show' through the use of visuals and action, rather than 'tell' through an over reliance on dialogue.

Redrafting is an essential part of the writing process; typically a screenplay will go through numerous drafts in the development period. This can mean changes to entire scenes, characters, dialogue or technical details. It's really helpful to read as many scripts as possible in order to learn the craft. The more you read the clearer the conventions of the format will become, which will allow you to concentrate on the content.

| – *Exercise* – |

Try setting your script idea out in the script format shown opposite.

In drama, in addition to the dialogue spoken by the actors, there are three techniques used to give further verbal information: Contextual, which is spoken or written at the beginning of a film in order to set up the story and provide background information (for example the **screen text** in *Star Wars* (1977)). Voice-over, which is spoken by one of the key characters at any time during the film providing insight into who they are and what they think (for example *Trainspotting* (1996)). And to camera, where a character can talk directly to the camera. This is known as 'breaking the fourth wall' because it breaks the screen convention by acknowledging the audience (for example *Alfie* (1966)).

Brutal Conviction – 2.

TV PRESENTER
Did you see anything suspicious on the night of the twentieth? Or do you know someone who did?…

9 INT. LOUNGE – BACK-ROOMS – WILEY SHOE-SHOP – NIGHT 9

The TV presenter is now an image on a TV screen….

TV PRESENTER
This fourth killing on the outskirts of the forest follows The same gruesome pattern as the last three murders. And all four bodies are as yet unaccounted for.

CHAD WILEY watches the TV as MADIE, his wife puts her coat on.

MADIE
I'm being picked up in a minute.

CHAD
Fine.

MADIE
There's some food if you're hungry.

CHAD
Whatever.

Her eyes glide towards the pile of shoe boxes in the corner.

MADIE
Chad?

No response. She watches him...he's in his own little world.

Her eyes fill with tears…it's unbearable. The doorbell rings.

10 INT/EXT. FRONT DOOR – HALL – WILEY SHOE-SHOP NIGHT

Madie opens the door. JAKE SUMMERS stands in the rain.

He smiles.

11 INT. LOUNGE – WILEY SHOE-SHOP – NIGHT

TV images of a press conference with a bereaved couple…

TV PRESENTER (V.O.)
At a press conference today, Clara Randall's mother told of her family's heartache at not knowing where their daughters body was buried.

Images of a map showing murder sites scattered around the forest...

TV PRESENTER (V.O.) (CONT'D)
Though police still suspect that they all lie buried within the heart of the forest itself.

Jake listens in.

JAKE
Looks like this area is famous at last.

Chad laughs and they shake hands heartily.

CHAD
Well how are you?

JAKE
Alright.

1. MAKING A KILLING SCRIPT PAGE
Style conventions followed include providing information about the setting in order to convey a sense of character through the environment they inhabit and centring dialogue on the page. A page of script equals approximately one minute of screen time.

A narrative is a story told in a specific way; the story that you choose to tell is unique to you. The way you see the world and how you communicate it is down to your particular perspective and those of the characters in your script. A story can be told by single or multiple characters, which can dramatically change the structure and atmosphere. In *Hero* (2002), we are given three versions of the same story within the course of the film. Each time it is made clear whose story we are seeing and how differently it has been told.

Much has been written about the way in which narrative structures operate. According to the **three act structure** the narrative is divided into three distinct sections. Act One is the beginning, where the story and characters are established. Act Two is the middle, where the story unfolds and develops. Act Three is the resolution, where the narrative strands are tied up. The end.

Drama arises from conflict and crisis. Often finding a character at an emotional crossroads that will change the rest of their life is a good starting point because it raises lots of questions and possible courses of action. The narrative unfolds from there with the results arising from the decisions and actions the character makes. The journey that follows may be emotional, psychological or physical but will leave the character in a different place to where they started.

Classic narrative operates to draw us through the story from beginning to end. An ongoing system of problems and solutions work to hold our interest and keep us guessing about what will happen in the end.

It is generally acknowledged that Act Two (the middle) presents the most problems to the writer because of the need to keep the audience engaged. To maintain interest, obstacles need to be placed in the path of the **protagonist,** which create further complications and conflict. An obstacle can be anything that creates a problem for the character; an argument with the boss, a bill that they can't afford to pay, missing the bus, etc. These are all events that will cause tension and extend the drama.

The narrative works by building tension and releasing it, which often subverts the audience's expectations. This technique is known as a twist. For example; the audience is led to think the argument with the boss will end in dismissal but, due to the twist, the boss has renewed respect for the employee for standing up to them and it actually results in a promotion.

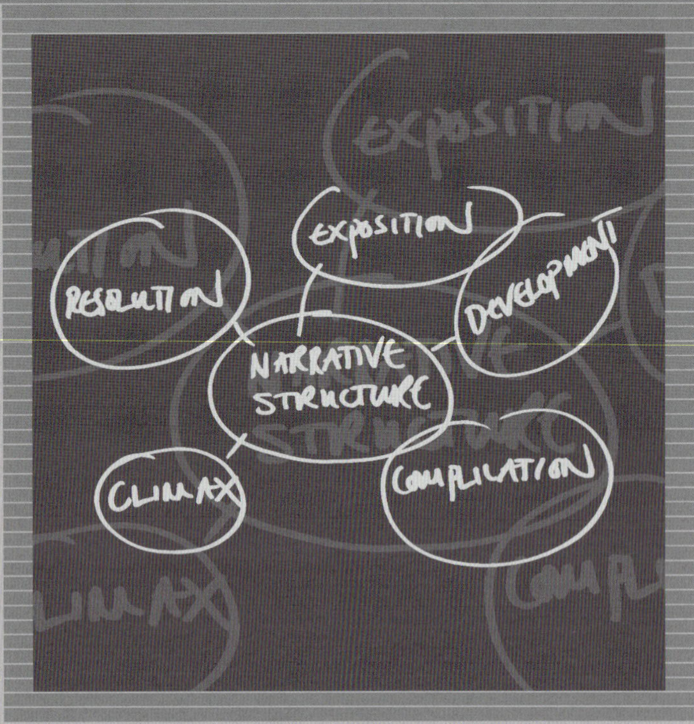

A simple storyline can be broken down into a five-step structure as follows:

1 **Exposition**
Opening premise. Setting the scene.

2 **Development**
The situation is built on and moves forward.

3 **Complication**
An event that changes the situation.

4 **Climax**
A decisive point when everything comes together.

5 **Resolution**
The outcome is reached.

Using *The Queen* (2006) as an example:

1 **Exposition**
Diana as an outsider to the Royal family.

2 **Development**
Princess Diana dies in a car crash.

3 **Complication**
The people protest at the Queen's lack of public sympathy putting the monarchy in crisis.

4 **Climax**
The Queen is forced to respond to media and public outcry.

5 **Resolution**
Normality is restored to the monarchy.

⌃ 1: FIVE-STEP STRUCTURE
Many stories have this simple five-step structure.

In the example used opposite the main story has been broken down. Often there will be several stories in any one film which form the overall structure. There will usually be at least one subsidiary storyline that intersects with the main one. This adds interest and can create added tension or intrigue by prolonging the resolution of the separate stories. For example, in *The Queen* (2006) the main story is concerned with the Queen's public response to Princess Diana's death. The subsidiary stories are about stalking and shooting a stag, and the complications arising from Tony Blair's spin on Diana's death.

The same five-step structure may be reconfigured depending on how film time is used, for example, in *Pulp Fiction* (1994) the film begins at the end. When thinking about narrative structure decisions have to be made as to whether the story unfolds in a linear or non-linear time sequence. Examples of non-linear time sequences are flashback, where we cut back and forth between the present and the past, and parallel storyline, which allows more than one story to be followed at any one time.

| – Exercise – |

Break down films you have seen recently into the five-step structure, from exposition through to resolution. Are some films more straightforward than others? You may find films with several storylines more complicated to unpick.

Even when there are flashbacks in a film they are portrayed through the context of the present tense. For example:

> ROBIN is sitting on a park bench thinking about the time he proposed to his ex-girlfriend.

There are two problems. Firstly, we cannot see what he is thinking. Secondly, he is remembering an event from the past but we cannot see it on-screen. This has to be made visible and captured on camera.

1 EXT. PARK BENCH. DAY.
ROBIN sits on a bench, chipping bits off the already peeling green paintwork.

2 EXT. PARK BENCH. DAY.
(FLASHBACK TWO YEARS EARLIER).
ROBIN goes down on one knee and looks up hopefully at LORNA. Before he can speak she jumps on him and they both fall over laughing and kissing.

3 EXT. PARK BENCH. DAY.
It starts to rain on ROBIN. He takes out his phone and dials LORNA.

1: RUN LOLA RUN
The use of a non-linear structure in *Run Lola Run* (1998) enhances the dramatic impact of the story and the three possible outcomes promote a sense of suspense.
Director: Tom Tykwer
Sony Pictures / The Kobal Collection

| – Exercise – |

Breakdown the last three films you've seen into the order of events portrayed on-screen. Consider how the structure is appropriate to the story. Does it enhance the tension as in *Run Lola Run* (1998)? Does it reinforce underpinning themes as in *Adaptation* (2002)?

A non-linear structure should enhance the story. For example, in *Run Lola Run* (1998), there are three different versions of events. Three alternative responses to the premise result in three possible conclusions. This ties in with the story – Lola has 20 minutes to get 100,000 Deutsch Marks to save her boyfriend from death. Thus the structure and the story work together to create a cohesive sense of what would happen should she choose a particular course of action.

Another example of structure supporting and enhancing the story can be seen in *Adaptation* (2002). The protagonist is struggling to adapt a novel to a screenplay and the film meanders and ponders on the character's self-doubt – nothing much happens. Halfway through, his twin brother attends a conference by scriptwriting guru Robert McKee, who advocates a tight narrative structure with action and dynamic characters responding to conflict. McKee's rules directly influence the second half of the film, which turns into an action-packed, classic plot-driven narrative. As a result the structure reinforces the story.

ARCHETYPAL STORIES

An archetype is an original that has been imitated, and in terms of stories it is claimed there are seven that often form the basis for all others. So although there appears to be an endless number of stories in the world, there are a limited number of archetypes – in other words, typical stories that are retold in different ways. The seven archetypes are: *Achilles*, *Cinderella*, *Circe*, *Faust*, *Orpheus*, *Romeo and Juliet* and *Tristan*. In the tale *Achilles*, for example, the character has one fatal flaw as in the original Greek myth. In the story of *Faust*, the character makes a pact with the devil, something that the protagonist is shown to do in *The Devil Wears Prada* (2006).

These stories recur in many films, books and even fairytales. Films often combine several of these types of stories – *The Departed* (2006), for example, is a combination of *Faust*, *Orpheus*, *Tristan* and *Circe*. These archetypes have resonance for film because they include underlying themes that are universal, such as the fatal flaw (*Achilles*), greed (*Faust*), love (*Romeo and Juliet*) and jealousy (*Tristan*).

1: ROMEO AND JULIET
Romeo and Juliet is one of the best known and most often used of the archetypal stories.

| – Exercise – |

Consider the last three films you have seen and apply one or more of the seven archetypal stories. You may be surprised by how easily many of the films you have seen are familiar and can be categorised using this method.

Some famous
protagonists vs antagonists

1 *Clarice Starling* *Dr Hannibal Lecter*
— ***The Silence of The Lambs*** **(1991)**

2 *Dorothy Gale* *The Wicked Witch*
— ***The Wizard of Oz*** **(1939)**

3 *Ellen Ripley* *The Alien*
— ***Alien*** **(1979)**

4 *Paul Sheldon* *Annie Wilkes*
— ***Misery*** **(1990)**

5 *I (Second Mrs de Winter)* *Mrs Danvers*
— ***Rebecca*** **(1940)**

6 *Snow White* *The Queen*
— ***Snow White and the Seven Dwarfs*** **(1937)**

7 *Jake Gittes* *Noah Cross*
— ***Chinatown*** **(1974)**

1: BUFFALO 66
In the film *Buffalo 66* (1998), Billy and Layla appear as an unconventional protagonist and antagonist.
Director: Vincent Gallo
Cinepix Film/The Kobal Collection

| – Exercise – |
Think about what motivates the protagonists in the list of protagonists opposite.

Clarice Starling wants to prevent murder.
Dorothy Gale wants to go home.
Ellen Ripley wants to destroy the alien.

Try finishing the list.

Protagonists and antagonists

The protagonist is the central character in a narrative (often the hero) whose actions propel the story forward. Usually the story is told from the perspective of the protagonist. The **antagonist** (often the villain) is the one who tries to prevent the protagonist from achieving their aim. The protagonist's actions tend to set a chain of events in motion, which the antagonist tries to disrupt in order to thwart the protagonist's intentions. This leads the protagonist to try a new course of action until a resolution is reached. The antagonist is not always human; it could be a force of nature. For example, in *Jaws* (1975) it is a shark and in *Cast Away* (2000) it is the island.

There are three classic protagonists: dramatic – succeeds due to his or her efforts (for example Dorothy Gale in *The Wizard of Oz* (1939)); tragic – fails in spite of his or her efforts (for example Jake Gittes in *Chinatown* (1974) and comic – succeeds in spite of his or her efforts (for example Harold Crick in *Stranger Than Fiction* (2006)).

The environment a character inhabits, their appearance, actions and the dialogue they use all provide information on personality, motivation and situation. Key characters should meet **internal** and **external conflict** through the course of the story. It is useful to limit the number of key characters and focus on giving them depth and credibility A complex character should have good and bad aspects to their personality making them credible and interesting.

MOTIVATION

Motivation is the reason behind a character's actions; it describes their aim. Big or small, there must be something that drives this aspect of the script, where the character has much to lose or gain. Motivation is usually comprised of a combination of personality and circumstance. Often we don't entirely appreciate a character's motivation until we learn about their past (in the **back story**). This tends to appear in the last quarter of the film, where information is revealed that keeps the narrative moving toward the resolution. The audience needs to be able to identify with the protagonist because their empathy is an important factor in sustaining interest in the film.

The character arc refers to the journey the protagonist takes during the film. This journey can lead to a process of change, where the character can be seen to develop. Think about the list of protagonists and antagonists on page 40 and consider how these protagonists change during the narrative. For example, Clarice Starling begins to empathise with the murderer and Dorothy Gale starts by wanting to leave home and finishes by realising 'there's no place like home'.

NAMES

A name can operate on numerous levels and can often provide clues about personality. A seemingly straightforward name can be a clever reference to a character or an aspect of the story. Popular television and film can help cement names as indicative of particular personalities. For example, the character Darcy in *Bridget Jones's Diary* (2001) is a reference to Mr Darcy in the novel *Pride & Prejudice*. You can use this to your advantage as a form of shorthand to inform the audience about the sort of person they are dealing with. This is something the Bond films do in particular as the female leads are often given names with sexual innuendo, a famous example being Pussy Galore. These standard expectations can be subverted by giving weak characters strong names and vice versa.

DIALOGUE

The dialogue should come late in the process after the structure, which acts as the foundation on which the rest of the script can be built. When writing dialogue it is essential to research your characters, especially if you are writing about a period, place or profession you do not have direct experience of.

A common mistake when starting out is to write too much dialogue. Every word should contribute to the character, narrative, or both, and dialogue should be pared down to the absolute essentials of short, succinct sentences in order to maintain interest and keep the pace flowing.

– Exercise –

Create a character profile. Think about who your character is; get to know them intimately. Decide on their history, including elements such as family, education and background. Then move into their present situation: where do they live, work and socialise? Practical and emotional details should be considered in order to create a character with sufficient depth.

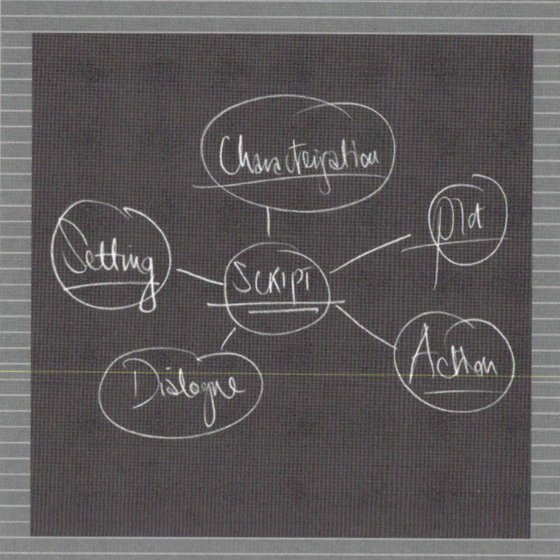

Film **adaptations** are based on an original text such as a novel or play, which is adjusted in order to fit the medium of film. Classics are often adapted for the screen, such as Shakespeare's plays or Dickens's novels. Recent examples include *The Lord of the Rings* trilogy from the novel by Tolkien, *Notes On A Scandal* by Zoë Heller and *Perfume* by Patrick Suskind.

When a novel is adapted for the screen a number of changes will be necessary; this is because some aspects of a novel cannot be achieved on-screen. In order to work, the script must be able to be seen and heard, which can cause problems for some film adaptations as often novels include the interior workings of a character's mind.

A complaint often voiced about adaptations by those who have read the original is that 'It's not as good as the book'. The point, however, is that an adaptation is always different. Often the film is loosely based on the book, retaining the spirit or essence rather than every detail. The other factor to be remembered about a film adaptation is that the reader of the book has already visualised the story, cast the characters in their mind and interpreted it according to their unique interior world. It is for this reason that the film adaptations of some novels are not always seen to be as powerful as the book.

1: SCRIPT
In order to create an effective script there are five essential elements that need to be considered: characterisation, plot, action, dialogue and setting. Without these, the script may appear weak.

⌃ 2: FILM ADAPTATIONS
Many films start life in the form of a novel. Often these films are loosely based on the book, retaining the spirit of the original as opposed to every detail.

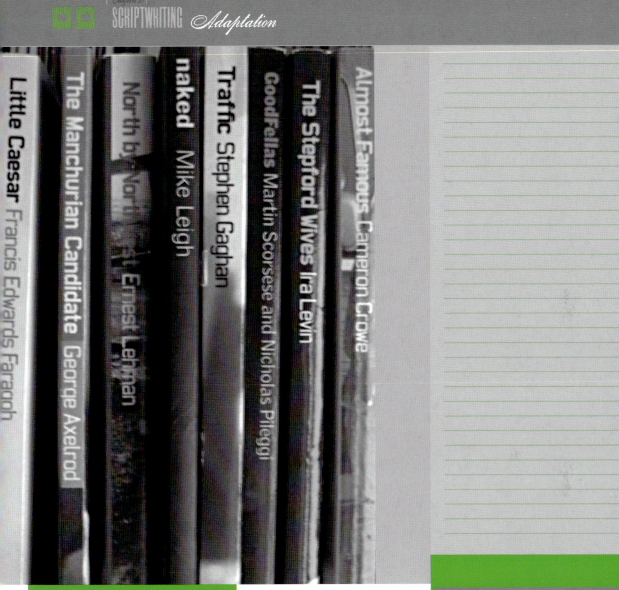

| – Exercise – |
Consider adaptations you have seen. What aspects were changed for the screen?

Genre is a French word meaning type or kind. The term is a quick way of categorising and identifying different types of films that possess similar plots, characters, settings and themes. Even if you've never heard of the term before you will have favourite genres. Do you always want to see action adventures, comedies or the latest animations when they come out? It is the genre that is drawing you to those choices.

In the Hollywood studio era, each of the studios was known for having a distinctive genre, which became part of their brand. For example, Warner Bros produced gangster, Ealing comedy and Hammer horror. Today it may not be quite as rigid, but genre remains a useful device in quickly identifying whether you want to see a film or not. By writing your script in a particular genre you are helping the audience to identify with key ideas in your story. That is not to say a rigid pattern or formula should be adhered to – by bringing individual creativity to your film, you can develop and add to the chosen genre.

The Searchers (1956), *Gunfight at the O.K. Corral* (1957), *Tombstone* (1993), *How The West Was Won* (1962) and *Unforgiven* (1992) all share similarities that we recognise as belonging to the western genre. The elements that are considered indicative of westerns are: they are usually set in pre-1900 on the American frontier, the heroes are pioneers in an untamed land and violent struggles with either Native Americans or outlaws result in triumph for the hero. Iconic props, costume and locations are all associated with a genre. In the western these include: saloon bars, horses, wagons, stagecoaches, the frontier landscape, the sheriff's office and cowboy hats.

Genre does not have to be a rigid, limiting factor on the film and can be used in many creative and playful ways. A sub-genre is a distinct variation on a genre, for example a spaghetti western (a sub-genre of a western), which retains some of the original elements of a western while adding new ones, such as big close-ups on faces, exaggerated camera angles, distinctive music and an element of black comedy. Many films combine genres, such as the popular romantic comedy. Other films incorporate three or more genres, such as *Blade Runner* (1982), which combines the characteristics of science fiction, thriller and film noir. *Scream* (1996) and *Scary Movie* (2000) both parody the genre conventions used in horror resulting in a horror comedy. These are just some of the ways in which genre can be used imaginatively in film.

⌃ *1:* HORROR GENRE
The visual iconography in films helps to identify the genre. In this horror example from *Making a Killing* (2002), there is the setting (forest), the costume (mask), the prop (knife) and the lighting (low-key).
Director: Ryan L Driscoll

| – *Exercise* – |

Identify the conventions that are usually found in the genres below. Consider setting, plot, characters, underpinning themes and visual iconography.

comedy
documentary
film noir
gangster
horror
musical
romance
science fiction
thriller

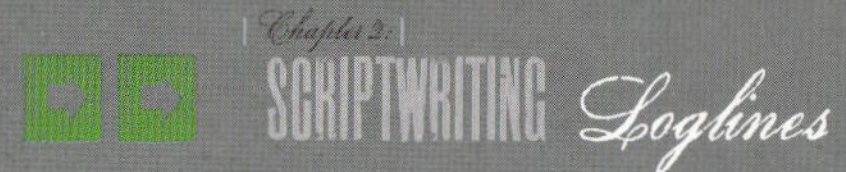

Scriptwriting Loglines

A logline is a sentence that captures the essence of what the film is about. It is used for publicity purposes to indicate the main thrust of the film. Without giving too much information away it teases the audience with a sense of what they can expect from the film. Some loglines are more effective and memorable than others. See how many of these you recognise.

Spider-Man 3 (2007)
The battle within.
How long can any man fight the darkness . . . before he finds it in himself?

Jaws 2 (1978)
Just when you thought it was safe to go back in the water.

E.T.: The Extra-Terrestrial (1982)
He is afraid. He is totally alone.
He is 3 million light years from home.

The Elephant Man (1980)
I am not an animal! I am a human being!
I . . . am . . . a man!

Notting Hill (1999)
Can the most famous film star in the world fall for just an ordinary guy?

Bridget Jones's Diary (2001)
It's Monday morning. Bridget has woken up with a headache, a hangover and her boss.

| – Exercise – |

Think about your script and consider the key points that capture and make it sound exciting and engaging. Have a go at writing a logline.

FAQs

Why write a treatment?
It will help you organise your material and can be used to apply for funding.

Why do I have to plan my script instead of just writing it?
If you don't plan it will take much longer to complete your script.

What if I don't want to have anything actually happen in my script?
Then perhaps you should write a novel.

Why do I have to research my script?
Research will help you to write credible characters and storylines that the audience can believe in.

If I am adapting an existing story what should I keep and what can I get rid of?
That depends on you and what you consider to be the crucial aspects of the original work.

—
Outline the key story events in a treatment.

—
Use standard screenplay format.

—
Take the audience on a journey.

—
Limit the number of characters and locations.

—
Structure your narrative, building and releasing tension.

—
Write visually – show not tell.

—
Use dialogue sparingly and thoughtfully.

—
Consider the practical implications of shooting your script.

Running glossary

Treatment/synopsis – summary of the story told in the present tense

Screen text – written information appearing on the screen

Three act structure – the beginning, middle and end of the story

Protagonist – the main character in the script

Antagonist – the opponent to the protagonist

Internal conflict – a problem within the character e.g. struggling with feelings of jealousy

External conflict – a problem outside the character e.g. an argument with another character

Back story – events that take place before the film begins

Adaptation – the reworking of a story in a medium different to its origin

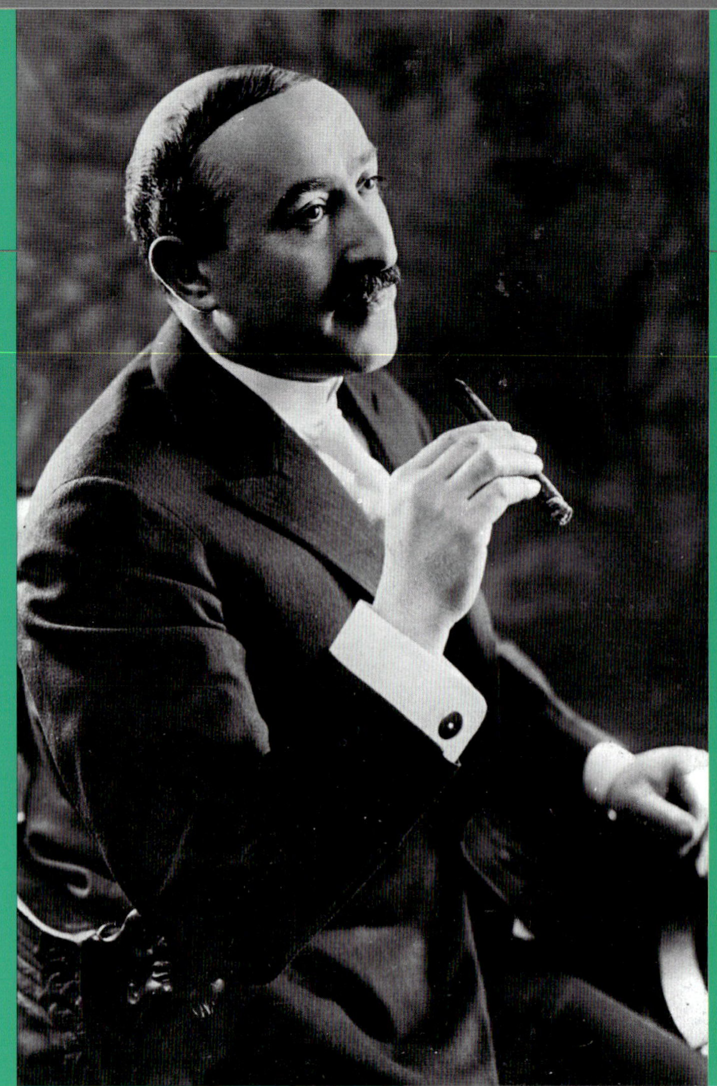

⌃ 1: THE PRODUCER
During the making of a film, it's the producer who calls the shots.
Getty Images

PRODUCING

The producer makes the project happen; they are responsible for assembling the cast and crew and negotiating their contracts. The production process begins with planning, whether making a drama or a documentary.

Production moves through three distinct phases. The first stage, pre-production, begins with funding, research and development. A **budget** and **schedule** are drawn up and a crew put together. The second phase is production, when the film is shot. The third is post-production editing, when music and special effects are added and rights are cleared. The whole process culminates in the distribution and exhibition of the finished film.

This chapter explains the production paperwork (covering legal requirements such as permissions, insurance and clearances – artist rights, copyright and archive) involved in getting organised for the shoot and making sure cast and crew are all kept informed of the plan. It will look at the essential organisation and administration that will enable the smooth running of the project from start to finish.

Production planning for documentary and drama

Drama works from a script with actors in constructed sets, while documentary generally relies on real people in real locations. Documentary doesn't just happen while the cameras are rolling; it is usually planned and scripted in advance. Very few documentaries are point and shoot – they have often been carefully researched with a clear story and characters in mind in the same way as a drama. In both cases the producers have a plan, which has been worked out during pre-production.

A shooting schedule and a budget are the two key responsibilities of the producer on any film, whether fact or fiction. From a director's shooting script (*see* Chapter 4) a schedule can be compiled. This is a list of shots from scenes set in the same location. They will be filmed in a block, which saves time and money by not having to travel backwards and forwards between locations. It is usual to film all the scenes set in one location before moving on to the next, thus films are normally shot out of chronological sequence.

FUNDING

Films screened in the cinema have received funding, which has paid for the cost of the production. There are a range of funding sources, which can generally be divided into either private or public funding. Public funding can come from government agencies, grants (in Britain: Arts Council, British Council, the UK Film Council and regional film offices), broadcasters (in Britain: BBC Films) and tax breaks. (*See* the Appendix for UK and international funding bodies.) Private funding can come from a company or individual who contributes to the production costs, usually in return for a percentage of the profits. Often films have more than one funding source, so you will see the names of several co-funders in the title sequence.

There are funds for different stages in the production, for example, development money at the beginning and completion money at the end. This funding structure recognises the different stages a film goes through and the importance of supporting the project throughout the entire production.

On 'low' to 'no budget' productions the film-makers may fund themselves. This results in a very tight budget, but the finished film can be used as a way of obtaining funding in the future. A major part of pre-production planning is working out a budget based on the available funds. To apply for funding for drama a treatment is written (*see* Chapter 2) and for documentary a proposal (*see* page 54).

1: FUNDING
There are various sources of funding available to film-makers, both in the private and public sectors.
Copyright: Teresa Pigeon

Documentary proposals

The proposal is a written bid aimed at securing financial backing. It includes a brief description of the purpose and the specifications of the project, explaining the subject of the documentary, what it is aiming to achieve and the target audience.

The proposal should summarise the content and key scenes of the documentary. It should be attention-grabbing and make whoever is reading it want to see the programme. As such it needs to suggest that the audience will see the intended subject from a different angle, learning or feeling something they didn't beforehand. A good proposal has a beginning, middle and end and takes the audience on a journey. It also includes strong characters with something to say.

There is no one rigid way of presenting the proposal, but there are general guidelines to help. It should be clear, concise and two or three pages in length. The first page should give the title, a short description and who it is aimed at (audience). The next pages should go into greater detail about the idea. Often the last page will include a paragraph on the key personnel who are attached to the project.

Access issues are fundamental to many documentaries so making clear who has agreed to participate in the documentary is very helpful. Someone may wish to make a documentary about Elizabeth Taylor but without her consent the idea is not going to become a reality.

SCRIPT BREAKDOWN

When the proposal is complete it is **pitched** to potential financiers. It should be remembered that the proposal is like a sales document – it is an attempt to convince people that the idea is worth making and a sound investment. Once funding is in place the next stage is the **script breakdown**.

The script is broken down into its production elements, which includes the locations, characters and props. A list is compiled of all the sets and locations, containing the scenes to be shot in each. From this the estimated number of shots in the film can be counted. A set-up is each time the camera is put in position to take a shot. Similar shots need to be grouped into a list of set-ups (thereby limiting the number of times to move and reposition the camera).

When the script has been broken down, the next stages are budgeting and scheduling. The budget should be based on the shooting script, which determines the number of days, locations, set ups per day and crew size required.

OUTLINE

This will be a documentary about stage fright that a rock band experiences before their official launch gig.

WORKING TITLE: Cold Feet   ESTIMATE TIME: 7 min

CONTEXTS OF THE SUBJECT

Stage fright or performance anxiety refers to an anxiety, fear or persistent phobia related to performance in front of an audience or camera. This form of anxiety can precede or accompany participation in any activity involving public self-presentation.

Performance anxiety is also observed in sportsmen. In the latter case it is interpreted as a fear to underperform (in view of the actual public or implied publicity).

Quite often stage fright arises in a mere anticipation of a performance, often long time ahead. It has numerous manifestations: fluttering or pounding heart, tremor in hands and legs, diarrhoea, facial nerve tics, dry mouth. Stage fright may be observed in ordinary people, beginning artists, as well as in accomplished ones. There are many tips on beating stage fright, but the worst enemy of stage fright is preparation.

No Verdict is a semi-professional versatile 5-piece covers band based in Kettering, Wellingborough. They play a variety of rock & pop from the 60's to the present day with a powerful guitar-driven sound with some twin-lead playing. Songs covered include bands such as The Beatles, Rolling Stones, Van Morrison, Bad Company, Free, T-Rex, The Sweet, Mud, The Who, AC/DC, Queen, Bon Jovi, Bryan Adams, ZZ Top, Guns 'n' Roses, The Darkness, The Kooks, The Feeling, Kaiser Chiefs, Razorlight, etc. They play for weddings & parties or pubs & clubs. They have their official launch gig on 17 Nov 2007. The band members include John Hickman (lead vocals), Michael Hickman (lead guitar), Tom Briggs (rhythm guitar), Paul Mason (bass guitar) and Neil Goulsbra (drums). Michael is school teacher in music in the daytime.

CHARACTERS & ACCESS

No Verdict members – contact through Michael who is my ex-housemate

ANGLE & INTENTIONS

Primary target audience will be people about age 15 - 45. The film is not initially to promote No Verdict. I would like to show that it's worth remembering that stage fright isn't necessarily a bad thing. It shows that you care about what you're doing and that it's a project that's actually worth getting scared about. Even really experienced people get stage fright every time, even ten, twenty, thirty years later. However, in consequence, this film would give the band good exposure to the audiences.

STYLE & STRUCTURE

The film will be an observational documentary that follows No Verdict's rehearsals and their official launch gig. The beginning will be an introduction of the band members and band's brief history. In the middle, the members talk about their stage experiences, especially about stage fright. This will be intersected by rehearsal scenes and their private life scenes to illustrate them juggling in their double life (e.g. teacher by day and rock'n'roller by the night) if appropriate. Towards the end, it shows tension and fear building up. On the gig night in the back stage, their nerves reach the climax. I will illustrate the fear through cinematic effects/techniques, music and comments from interviews. The film ends with the members' overall thoughts after the stage.

I am thinking finishing the film by putting a No Verdict music video made with footage from the gig after the main feature.

LOCATION LIST

Rehearsal studio   Members' homes

Gig venue   Members' workplaces

Town of Kettering, Wellingborough

POSSIBLE MEDIA FOR THE FILM TO BE SHOWN

Websites – You Tube, Four Doc, My Space

Short film festivals

1: DOCUMENTARY PROPOSAL
The proposal should clearly indicate the nature of the story and style of the film.
Student film-maker: Momoko Abe

Budgeting

The cost of making a film can vary from production to production, but whatever the cost it is important to create a budget. Having a checklist of all possible costs helps to create a realistic budget to work from. Once the budget is defined it becomes a blueprint for the production of the film.

The budget is fundamental to the film that will be made; how much money you have available to produce the script will influence the end product enormously. For example, *LA Takedown* (1989) and *Heat* (1995) were produced from the same script. However, *LA Takedown* was made for TV production while *Heat* was for cinema release, thus it had a much bigger budget to play with.

Having a big budget will not necessarily result in a great film. There are many examples of films that have failed in spite of funding, such as *Waterworld* (1995) and *The Avengers* (1998). This reveals weaknesses in other aspects of the project; sometimes the script is not ready to go into production, or the wrong director or actors are chosen.

Having a limited budget can actually be an advantage as creative solutions have to be found to solve problems, which can result in innovative and exciting film-making at its best. This can be seen in *The Blair Witch Project* (1999) and *The Full Monty* (1997).

Decisions have to be made about how the available budget will be divided between the different departments and their needs. So, for example, one producer might carve up the budget in favour of paying for a big star in the hope that they will attract a wider audience to see the film; while another producer might put that money into making the film look stunning in terms of design, lighting or photography.

'Above the line' refers to the portion of the budget that includes the producer, director, stars, script and writers – the creative elements. 'Below the line' refers to crew and craft costs – the production elements.

Costs to be considered in the budget will vary depending on the type and scale of the project. Generally speaking most will include: cast and crew, equipment hire, tape stock, location or studio fees and travel and subsistence. All productions need public liability insurance and equipment insurance. In addition to these costs a percentage of the budget is always set aside for contingency, which will cover any unforeseen costs that may occur.

Some more specific costs may include: rights acquisitions – buying the rights to produce a film from the person who wrote it. Music clearance – if copyrighted music is included in the film it must be cleared and paid for before it can be legally used. Archive footage clearance – using anything created by other people will need to be cleared and paid for.

PRODUCTION BUDGET		Title :	Prod Ref:	
BUDGET ALLOCATION	RESEARCH	PRODUCTION	POST PROD.	CONTINGENCY
RESOURCES		REQUIREMENT	RATE	CIST
Director				
Production manager				
Production Assistant				
Researcher				
Designer				
Script				
Camera Operator				
Sound/Boom Operators				
Equipment				
Electrician				
Lighting				
Studio				
Location Fees				
Construction				
Costume Hire				
Props Hire				
Actors				
Tape Stock				
Editor				
Offline Edit				
Offline Tapes				
Online Edit				
Master Tape				
Voice-over Artist				
Voice-over Recording				
Graphics				
Library Music				
Original Music				
Travel/Transportation				
Accommodation				
Subsistence				
Telephone				
Insurance				
Petty Cash				
Admin				

⌃ 1: BUDGET SHEET
Making the figures in the budget add up is a major part of producing, and the budget sheet is an invaluable tool for this.

| – Exercise – |

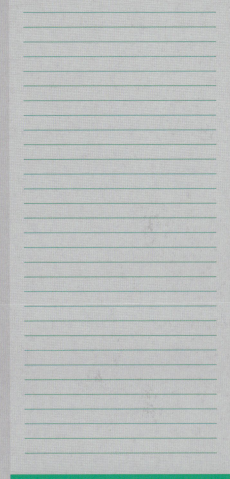

Watch *LA Takedown* (1989) and *Heat* (1995) and make a list of all the differences. Next to each of your points write down whether you think it is budget related or not.

Schedules

The making of a film can take anything from a day to several months depending on the length and complexity of the script.

The schedule breaks the shoot into a day-by-day plan of what will be shot and how many days it will take to complete the film. A backup plan, known as a contingency, is an important part of any schedule. For example, if bad weather interrupts an exterior day of shooting a contingency plan will be needed so that alternative shooting can take place.

Schedules are drawn up in relation to how many scenes can be filmed each day; they break down the scenes from a script into location and character groupings. The aim is to shoot everything in a particular location before moving on to the next one in order to save time and money. Likewise, by taking into account which characters are required for each scene, all of an actor's scenes can be shot together so that they are not on-set all day with one scene at the beginning and one at the very end. To have an actor waiting around all day unnecessarily would be bad scheduling as they would have to be paid for their time.

Another factor to consider when scheduling is the location, that is, whether shooting will take place in exterior locations or in studio interiors. The studio is a controlled environment while the location is not and so presents possible interruptions caused by weather, people, noise and traffic. Extra time is factored into the schedule for location filming. The number of cast and possible camera movements also need to be considered when scheduling extra time allocation.

Any item that affects the time taken to complete the shot should be considered when drawing up the schedule. The daylight hours and weather forecasts are consulted as a guide to help calculate how long each shooting day will be.

CALL SHEETS

From the overall schedule a daily schedule, known as a **call sheet**, is drawn up. This is distributed to all crew and cast members and details the key information for each day of filming. It includes: the call time – when everyone is expected to arrive on-set; contact details of all the crew; the intended scenes to be shot and in what order that day; details of how to get to the locations and the wrap time – the time the shoot will end.

– NEW SCHEDULE 2ND MAY

BRUTAL CONVICTION | **SHOOTING SCHEDULE** | **SHOOT DAY 1**

02/05/00 TUES | LOCATION - THEYDON BOIS | SUNSET - | CALL - 12.30PM
BASE - MONYASH, SYDNEY ROAD | WRAP - 10.30PM
EMERGENCY NO: 07931 842782

SCENE	I/E	D/N	SETTING/ DESCRIPTION	CHARACTERS	PROPS	NOTES/ FX
11A	INT	DAY	PRESS CONFERENCE	BEREAVED COUPLE	MURDER SITES MAP	REPORTER'S SUITS
				REPORTERS	CAMERAS/ FLASHES	
				DC NEAL	MIKES/ BOOMS	
					JUG OF WATER	
					GLASSES	
					SCREENS/ POSTERS	
19	INT	NT	HALLWAY - JAKE'S FLAT	MADIE	TELEPHONE	
			MADIE RUSHES TO PHONE			
21	INT	NT	UPSTAIRS LANDING - JAKE'S FLAT	MADIE		
			MADIE MARCHES UPSTAIRS			
23	INT	NT	UPSTAIRS LANDING - JAKE'S FLAT	MADIE	MASK	
			MADIE LOOKS DOWNSTAIRS/ATTACKE	MASKED FIGURE	LEATHER GLOVES	
27	INT	NT	UPSTAIRS LANDING - JAKE'S FLAT	JAKE	BLOOD	
			JAKE FOLLOWS TRAIL OF BLOOD			
26	INT	NT	HALLWAY - JAKE'S FLAT	JAKE	BLOOD	
			JAKE ENTERS/ SEES TRAIL OF BLOOD...			
22	INT	NT	JAKE'S BEDROOM - JAKE'S FLAT	MADIE	TELEPHONE	
			MADIE TRIES PHONE/ WALKS OUT		W/ CUT LINE	
24	INT	NT	JAKE'S BEDROOM - JAKE'S FLAT	MADIE	KNIFE	BLOOD ON MADIE?
					BLOOD	
28	INT	NT	JAKE'S BEDROOM - JAKE'S FLAT	JAKE	BLOOD (LOADS)	CORPSE MAKE-UP
				MADIE (CORPSE)	MIRROR	BLOODIED ROOM
				MASKED FIGURE	TELEPHONE	W/ PALM-PRINTS
41	INT	NT	JAKE'S BEDROOM - JAKE'S FLAT	JAKE	BLOODY BED	
			JAKE IMAGINES BED OF BLOOD			
105	INT	NT	JAKE'S BEDROOM - JAKE'S FLAT	MADIE		
			JAKE IMAGINES MADIE TURNING			
107	INT	NT	JAKE'S BEDROOM - JAKE'S FLAT	MADIE	KNIFE	
			JAKE IMAGINES MADIE KNIFED		BLOOD	
109	INT	NT	JAKE'S BEDROOM - JAKE'S FLAT	MADIE	BLOOD	
			JAKE IMAGINES MADIE HIT BED			
111	INT	NT	JAKE'S BEDROOM - JAKE'S FLAT	MASKED FIGURE	BLOOD	MASK
			MASKED FIGURE LUNGES AT JAKE			KNIFE
104	INT	DAY	JAKE'S BEDROOM - JAKE'S FLAT	JAKE	BLOOD	PRINTS ON WALL
			JAKE FILMS MURDER SCENE		CAMCORDER	
					BLOODY MATTRESS	
106	INT	DAY	JAKE'S BEDROOM - JAKE'S FLAT	JAKE	BLOOD	PRINTS ON WALL
			JAKE CONTINUES TO FILM		CAMCORDER	
					BLOODY MATTRESS	
108	INT	DAY	JAKE'S BEDROOM - JAKE'S FLAT	JAKE	BLOOD	PRINTS ON WALL
			JAKE STRUGGLES TO CONTINUE		CAMCORDER	
					BLOODY MATTRESS	
110	INT	DAY	JAKE'S BEDROOM - JAKE'S FLAT	JAKE	BLOOD	PRINTS ON WALL
			JAKE COLLAPSES ON BED		CAMCORDER	
					BLOODY MATTRESS	

Call Sheet : Brutal Conviction

Production Office
18 Hastings Ave
Barkingside
Ilford
Essex
IG6 1DZ

Tel: 020 8551 8455

Date: SAT 6th MAY 2000
Unit Call: 9 AM
Meet At: BASE : MONYASH SYDNEY ROAD.

Shoot Day: 5
Sunrise: EARLIER THAN YOU'LL WAKE UP
Sunset: 8.45 ish.

Director: Ryan Lee Driscoll (Mob: 07931 842782)
Production Manager: Enara A. Lariz (Mob: 07957 650493)

Weather: OF THE SUNBATHING KIND

1st AD: Justin Murphy (Mob: 07970 077460)

Sc. No	I/E	D/N	Location	Action	Cast*	Pgs
97, 164, 201	I	D	INTERROGATION ROOM	POLICE WATCH VIDEOS	N, R	3/8
29, 261, 263, 265, 298	I	D		JAKE QUESTIONED RE. MADIE + JAKE'S INTERROGATION	N, R, J	2 2/8
274, 276	I	D		CHAD ANGRY + FIGHTING JAKE	J, C, D, R, N	7/8
254	I	N		DI ASKS WHERE BODIES ARE HID	J, R, N	2/8
267/269	I	N		JAKE EXPLAINS PLOT	J, R, W, PC,	1 4/8
273, 275, 268, 270	I	D, N	BEHIND 2-WAY	POLICE WATCHING/DISCUSSING JAKE	J, R, G, N, C	6/8
147	I	N	BATHROOM	CHAD WITH RAZOR BLADE	C	1/8
167	I	N	HOSPITAL ROOM	CHAD IN HOSPITAL	J, C, NURSE	5/8

*Cast	Character	Actor	M/U & W/D	On Set
N	D.C. NEAL	DAVID McCAFFREY.	9 AM	9.30 AM
R	D.I. RAWLINGS	GREGORY COX	9 AM	9.30 AM
J	JAKE	HYWEL MORGAN	10 AM	10.30 AM
C	CHAD	SEAN GALLAGHER	3 PM	3.30 PM
D	P.C. DOUGLAS	RAY NEWE	3 PM	3.30 PM
W	ALICE WITHAM	SARAH RICE	4.30 PM	5.00 PM
PC	PC AVERY	LINDSAY CARR	4.30 PM	5.00 PM
G	GLARIN	PAUL HURSFIELD	5.30 PM	6.00 PM
Nurse	Nurse !	ONE LUCKY CREW MEMBER.		

Breakfast At: | **Lunch At:** 2 PM. | **Dinner At:**

2nd Location Address: N/A. | **Location Move At:**

Action Props:

Special Notices:

Checked By: Prod. Man: | 1st AD: | 2nd AD:

1: SHOOTING SCHEDULE
The schedule breaks the shoot down into a day-by-day plan. It details what will be shot, in what order and over how many days.

2: CALL SHEET
The call sheet is a breakdown of the shooting that is to take place that day. It is based on the shooting schedule.

Locations

Shooting usually takes place in a combination of real locations and studio-built settings. There are advantages and disadvantages to both. When using a real location, a **recce** is carried out. On a recce practical considerations like the available light and accessible power points for equipment are noted. Possible problems, such as any sort of activities that may interfere with filming, are identified. These could include noise from traffic if the location is near a busy road, or noise from aeroplanes if the location is on a flight path. Potential crowd control issues can also prove to be problematic.

Photographs are taken on the recce so that other departments can see the location and discuss whether it is appropriate for the shoot.

The following checklist is a useful guide when carrying out a recce:

— Look at and take pictures of the location.

— Visit at the same time of day you intend on shooting.

— Talk to people on the spot.

— Locate electricity supplies.

— Consider sources of sound interference.

— Confirm shooting permissions.

— Consider logistics of transport, parking, toilets and catering.

If shooting exteriors, an alternative interior shot should be set-up as a contingency in case of bad weather.

Permission must be obtained from the location before a shoot can take place. The property may be privately owned or owned by the council. The relevant people who will be able to authorise the shooting and sign the permissions forms must be contacted prior to the shoot with the dates and times of filming agreed in advance. Location issues to be considered include: health and safety, and liaising with the police and the local council film officer.

Health and safety procedures on-location and in the studio help to ensure safe practice for cast, crew and the public. A risk assessment form is filled in identifying all possible hazards in each place of shooting. This covers everything from entrance and exit points to fire prevention and regulations.

If a shoot is set-up without gaining prior permission there is the risk that it will be closed down by the police. No permit, no film.

LOCATION INDEMNITY FORM

NAME OF PROPERTY: ______________________

ADDRESS OF PROPERTY: ______________________

____

DATE: ______________________

RE: ______________________ ("the property")

("us") write to confirm our agreement as follows:-

1. You, hereby, grant to us and persons authorised by us (and warrant that you are entitled to grant to us) the sole and exclusive/non-exclusive right during the Period to enter upon the Property and to film, photograph and record the Property and for such purpose to bring onto the Property such persons and equipment as necessary
2. "The Period" shall mean (i) ______________ and (ii) such other days or half days as we may mutually agree.
3. All rights in the films, photographs and recordings made and/or taken by us at the property shall vest in us and we shall be entitled to assign, license and/or exploit the same by all means and in all media as we may at our absolute discretion elect and without any entitlement to you to share in any remuneration thereof. We shall be entitled to refer to the Property by its true name or by a fictitious name or not to refer to the Property by name and shall have no obligation to you to include any or all of such films, photographs, recordings or transmissions in any films or programme or to exploit the same or any film or programme in which the same are included.
4. ______________ shall indemnify you against any damage which may be caused to the Property by the negligent act or omission of ourselves or our agents, employees or invitees.
5. This agreement shall be freely assignable by us and shall be interpreted in accordance with the laws of England.

Kindly indicate your acceptance of the foregoing by signing and returning to us the enclosed duplicate of this letter.

Yours Faithfully	Read and Agreed by
	(PRINT NAME)
	(SIGN)
For and on behalf of	duly authorised for and on behalf of
and	______________ the owner

1: LOCATION RECCE
During a recce, photographs are taken of the proposed location. These are then shared with other members of the team so that decisions on the appropriateness for the shoot can be made.

2: LOCATION INDEMNITY FORM
A location indemnity form must be signed by the owner of the property that is intended to be used for the shoot. Without this, filming cannot be carried out.

Equipment

There is an extensive range of equipment required when making a film. It would be impractical to purchase all of this equipment every time, therefore it is often hired from specialist companies called facilities houses. Facilities houses are devoted to equipment hire for film-making, which includes a range of lighting, cameras and their attachments, such as dolly, track and cranes.

It is usual for the director of photography (DOP) to draw up a list of equipment requirements based on the script and following discussions with the director and producer. Again, budget will determine whether they can afford to hire everything they think is necessary, for as many days as they would like.

There is a rate of hire for each item of equipment, which is taken into account in the budget. Whatever equipment is hired requires insurance in case of damage or theft. Post-production facilities costs will also need to be included in the budget.

equipment rentals (production)

DAY/WKND	
DIGITAL VIDEO CAMERA	
$100/$150	Canon GL-1: miniDV format; LCD viewscreen; 20X zoom; three CCD chips; beachtek XLR inputs; image stabilization; 16:9 mode; 2 batteries; Tiffen filter set; more features
16MM SYNC SOUND CAMERAS	
$125/$175	Arri SR package: Zeiss 10-100mm; (2) 400' mags; (2) batteries; charger; handgrip; 3x3 Matte Box; changing bag; fluid head tripod; additional accessories made available through Lee Utterbach Camera
$80/$100	CP16R package: Orientable reflex viewfinder; 12-36fps; 144° shutter (ideal for shooting TV screens); 12-120 Angenieux zoom; (2) 400' mags; (2) batteries; changing bag; Bogen fluid-head tripod
$70/$90	CP16A packages: same package accessories as above; non-orientable viewfinders; 24 f.p.s. only
16MM NON-SYNC CAMERAS	
$65/$80	Arri S package: 9.5-95mm zoom; var. speed motor; (2) 400' mags; battery; changing bag; pin registered
$55/$65	EBM Electric Bolex w/Crystal package: crystal 24fps and 10-50fps var. speed motor; 10mm, 25mm, 75mm prime lenses; (2) 400' mags; battery; changing bag
$40	Spring Bolex (Rex 5) w/Zoom: 12-64 var. speed motor; 12-120mm Angenieux zoom
$40	Spring Bolex w/Primes:12-64 var. speed motor; 10mm, 25mm, 75mm prime lenses
CAMERA ACCESSORIES	
$15each	Bolex Lenses: 5.9mm, 10mm, 16mm, 50mm macro, 150mm
$20each	Arri Lenses: Cooke 37.5mm, 75mm, 100mm; Schneider 10mm, 75mm; Kilar 90mm macro;
$35	O'Connor 50 Fluid Head Tripod, spreader, and baby legs
$25	NCE Fluid Head Tripod: w/hi-hat, spreader
$25	Bogen Fluid Head Tripod
$10	Bogen Friction Head Tripod
$20	Hi-hat: O'Connor Model C
$10	Sekonic Light Meter: reflective and incident light readings
$15	Cable Release: for Spring Bolex
$10	400' Magazine: for ESM motor or EBM Electric Bolex
$10	Pistol Grip: for Spring Bolex
$10	Shoulder Brace
$5/each	Slate

1: EQUIPMENT RENTAL
There are numerous facilities houses that can be called upon to hire specialist film-making equipment. This can include lighting, cameras and camera attachments.

FILM AND TAPE STOCK

The choice of shooting format will influence the budget and schedule because digital video tape is more economical and faster to use than film.

Shooting on film offers a diverse choice of stock, which responds differently to light. Film stocks vary in several ways, including where they should be used (inside with tungsten light or outside with daylight), speed (high, medium and low), their size (Super 8, 16mm or 35mm) and how they reproduce colour. The choice of stock can change the film from looking grainy and realistic, to beautiful and dream-like.

Digital video refers to any camcorder that makes a digital recording rather than an analogue one. This covers the range of formats from the high-end ones used by professionals (Digibeta, DVCPRO and High Definition) through to domestic camcorders.

The DOP will usually test a variety of film stock and formats out before production begins in order to find the desired effect for the project. They may combine a range of stocks to create different looks at different stages of the film.

2: FILM AND TAPE STOCK
Films can be shot either digitally or on film. There are advantages and disadvantages to both formats.
Copyright: Valerie Loiseleux

Distribution and exhibition

The producer makes deals with distributors and sales agents to sell the rights to different territories internationally. Nationally the distribution can be broken down into broadcast, theatrical, home entertainment and the Internet. The producer will usually take the finished product to film markets and festivals, such as Cannes and Milan, to secure distribution and exhibition. This should also be included in the budget with publicity and marketing costs.

RELEASE FORMS

A **release form** is an agreement signed by anyone who appears in the film. Release forms vary considerably from production to production but the key point is that the contributor signs the form agreeing to the use of the footage shot of them. This permission is important, as without it their contribution cannot be included in the film.

STANDARD FORM OF CONSENT

PROGRAMME TITLE:

EPISODE NUMBER AND SUB-TITLE:

DATE OF RECORDING/PERFORMANCE:

To:
Address:

(i) I confirm that I have agreed to contribute to or participate in the above recording as agreed with ____________ and/or ________ ________ representative;

(ii) I hereby give all consents and permissions and grant any and all rights that may be required under any legislation or regulation throughout the world to permit my contribution/performance to be used in whole or in part in any manner whatsoever by ____________ and/or ____ ____________ in all media worldwide in perpetuity without restriction and without any right to receive any remuneration in connection therewith.

Name of Contributor: ____________

Signed: ____________ Date:

Address: ____________

____

Postcode: ____________ Telephone: ____________

Where the contributor is under 18 years of age, I confirm that I am the parent/guardian and agree my acceptance of the above on behalf of the contributor

Signed: ____________ Date: ____________

Address: ____________

1: FORM OF CONSENT
A consent or permission form must be signed by everyone appearing in front of the camera. Without this, the footage cannot be used.

FAQs

Do I need funding for a student project?
If you have access to equipment and facilities as part of your course it is possible to make the film with limited costs. You will still need to account for travel and any props or costumes.

What if I don't have a crew?
Depending on the scale of the project it may be possible to make the film yourself. If that is too big a task you could ask friends or post an advert on one of the many websites, such as Shooting People (shootingpeople.org).

Why do I have to do a budget?
This is an important part of getting organised and ensuring that you spread available funds across the project and don't run out of money before the film is finished.

Why do I need a schedule – can't I just make it up as I go along?
The schedule will make sure you use your time effectively, providing a plan to work to and saving time in the long run.

How can I become a producer?
Learn about film and about finance. Talk to producers and get advice.

—
Producing requires strong negotiating skills – shop around and get the best prices available.

—
Costs can be kept down by limiting the number of locations and the distance between them.

—
Shooting on a digital format rather than film will be cost-effective.

—
Keeping crew size to a minimum will also save money.

—
Using available light where possible will cut down on the cost of lighting hire.

Running glossary

Budget – the money available for the project

Schedule – the time available for the project

Pitching – presenting the film concept in a succinct and appealing fashion in order to convince others to either commission or fund it

Script breakdown – the script is divided into components such as scenes and locations, all grouped together accordingly for shooting purposes

Call sheet – a daily document stating where and when shooting will take place

Recce – short for 'reconnaissance', meaning visiting all of the shooting locations in advance and making notes of the positive and negative features

Release form – also known as a consent form, signed by those appearing in the film

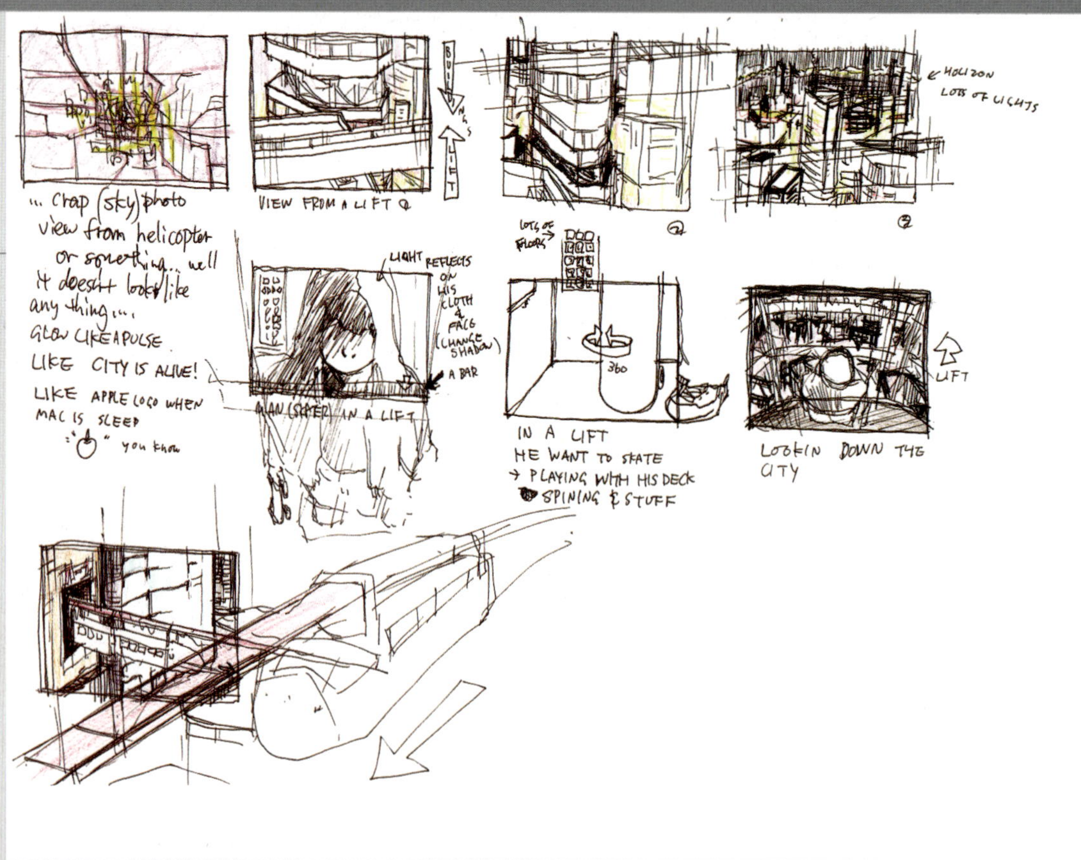

1: STORYBOARD
Storyboards are an important tool to help the director visualise the script. Storyboards do not have to be artistically perfect; they just need to convey the relevant information to the team.
Director: Lucia Helenka

4 DIRECTING

The director decides on the look and feel of a film; they are responsible not only for where the camera will be in relation to the action but also how the actors perform in front of it. The process begins when they read the script and form a stylistic approach to the material. During pre-production the director draws up **storyboards** and shooting scripts, which describe on paper how the script will be shot.

When a director first imagines the script they are likely to see many different ways of filming it. The practical considerations of time and money (*see* Chapter 3) will impact on what can be achieved and their vision must be tailored to these. This chapter explains the building blocks necessary for the making of the film; shot sizes and movement and the way in which these can be selected and combined, culminating in the creation of the storyboards and shooting script.

Shot sizes – meaning and motivation

Before shooting can begin the director breaks the script down into the separate shots they will use to tell the story. This choice is based on an understanding of film language, where each shot is used for a particular purpose. Shot sizes describe the distance from the camera to the object/subject, ranging from close-up to long shot. This physical description also communicates psychological messages to the audience.

The closer the shot, the more specific detail is picked out and the greater the intimacy. How many people in life do we see close enough to check out their blackheads or nasal hair? However, when you are this close you lose contextual information, such as costume, body language and environment.

The further out the shot, the more contextual information is gained, but the fine detail of facial expression, emotional response, and so on, will be lost.

Shot composition is concerned with how objects are positioned in the frame. The visual components communicate ideas and emotions in the script and are decided on in close discussion with the designer (*see* Chapter 5) and the director of photography (DOP) (*see* Chapter 6).

1: BCU
Big close-up. Head or part of head. This is useful to show emotion and detail. Reserved for passion or conflict.

Shot sizes – meaning and motivation

2: CU
Close-up or close shot.
Head and shoulders. Reveals character personality. Intimate and powerful. Useful for dramatic or revealing moments of truth/crisis. Close shots work to increase audience identification with a character.

3: MCU
Medium close-up.
Top pocket.
Useful all round shot.

4: MS
Mid shot. To waist. This shot provides information on the body language and clothes of the character.

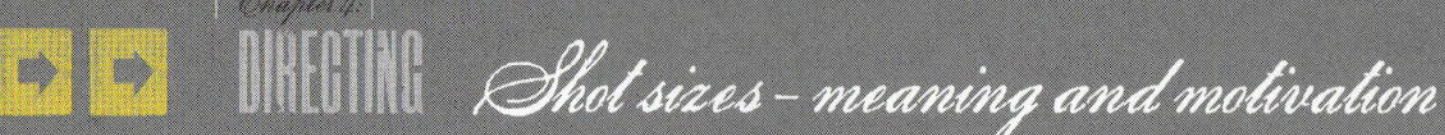

Shot sizes – meaning and motivation

5: MLS
Medium-long shot. Including the knees. Provides more physical information than the mid shot, but less close detail.

6: LS
Long shot. Full figure. Contextualises characters in their locations. This can often be used to distance the audience from events or suggest loneliness or isolation.

7: WS
Wide shot. Master or establishing shot. Establishes location often used at the beginning of a scene and again at the end. It helps make clear the physical geography of the space and sets up atmosphere.

Shot sizes – meaning and motivation

8: O/S
Over the shoulder. This helps create a dynamic between the character and what they are seeing. Can also be used to suggest someone is being followed or watched by an unseen presence.

9: 2/S
Two shot (three shot and so on). By framing two or more characters in the same shot a sense of how they relate to each other is created. The opposite of this is to keep characters in separate frames to suggest a lack of common ground or interaction.

10: POV
Point of view. Provides perspective from a particular character's view. The director manipulates whose eyes the audience experience the story from.

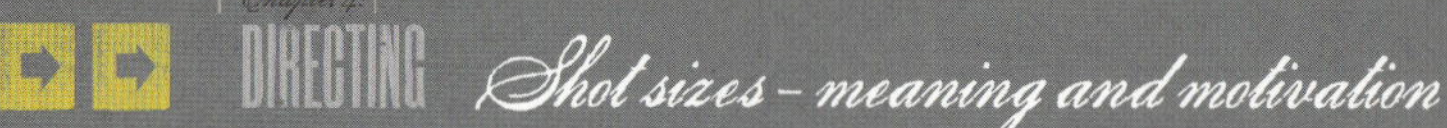

Shot sizes – meaning and motivation

⌃ 11: **HIGH ANGLE**
Camera from above eyeline pointing down. Looking down on someone. Indicates low status or vulnerability of some sort.

⌃ 12: **LOW ANGLE**
Camera below eyeline pointing up. Indicates high status – someone powerful or scary.

⌃ 13: **DUTCH ANGLE**
Camera is deliberately at a diagonal angle, which is used to disorientate as in *The Third Man* (1949).

Shot sizes – meaning and motivation

1 – 2: HIGH ANGLE
Placing the camera at a high angle in the first shot creates a sense of vulnerability and isolation. In the second high-angle shot, the impression of seeing something that shouldn't be seen is given.

3 – 4: SHOT/REVERSE
In these two shots, the characters appear to be looking at each other through the window. This allows a point of view to be created, whereby the audience sees what the characters see.

| – Exercise – |

To help you think about how the camera can be used to tell a story, read the brief below and consider how best to convey the variables.

A powerful/weak person enters a room and in an angry/sad mood addresses the room anxiously/ecstatically.

Camera movements – methods and meaning

The director needs to consider movement when filming as its introduction adds another dimension to the grammar of the shot. Close attention to focus is required when the camera and/or the subject is mobile. The speed of movement dramatically affects the impression and can add resonance to a shot. For example, a slow pan creates a different effect to a whip pan – the first being used to soothe, the second to jolt or startle the viewer.

These movements have a significant effect on the relationship between the subject and the camera. The tracking shot, for example, is considered to increase the perception of depth, which can be an effective tool. However, realist film-makers, such as Jean-Luc Godard, have rejected tracking, considering it to be artificial and less honest than a static camera. Tracking can also be irritating and unnecessary to the intended meaning of the scene, for example, when the 360-degree track around a character is overused, often for no particular reason.

1: WINGS OF DESIRE
In this scene from *Wings of Desire* (1987) the camera height and movement involve the audience in the interior world of the trapeze artist.
Road Movies/Argos/WDR/
The Kobal Collection

Camera movements – methods and meaning

Pan
The camera head moves from side to side from a fixed position on the horizontal axis. We are put in the position of the character, for example, looking from left to right, and given a privileged position being able to follow action and see details as they are revealed.

Tilt
The camera head moves up or down from a fixed position on the vertical axis. Can be used to reveal such things as how tall a building is or someone about to jump from the roof of it.

Zoom in or out
The lens on the camera adjusts the distance but the camera stays still. The zoom widens or narrows the angle, cuts out more of the background and limits the depth of field. Zooming in makes the image look bigger; zooming out makes the image look smaller. The human eye doesn't zoom.

Track in or out
The camera itself moves towards or away from the subject. This allows a close following of the action, creating a dynamic flow.

Tracking into a subject creates a different effect to tracking out. In contrast to the zoom, a track allows more background in the shot but requires refocusing.

Dolly
Dolly shots – in which the camera is mounted on wheels – involve us in the scene, taking us physically in and out and creating the impression of depth.

Crane
Attaching the camera to a crane allows it to swoop down and soar up, creating distance and drama.

Hand-held
Is a dynamic movement, often used to follow live action for documentary. Used less in drama as it can be shaky and unstable.

Steadicam
Is a piece of equipment that is attached to the operator. The shock absorbers allow very flexible natural movement without the instability of hand-held shots.

| – *Exercise* – |

Try shooting a simple scene, such as someone walking along a street, using each of the movements described exclusively.

How does the movement influence the meaning? Which seems the most effective choice and why?

Master shots, cutaways, inserts and reactions

When breaking down a scene the director must consider the main guidelines that help convey the action. Films in the early days of cinema consisted of a single shot. The camera was set in a static position and recorded what was in front of it. This is known as a master shot because it is a wide frame that shows everything in the scene. Today a master shot is usually used at the beginning of a scene before moving into a range of other shots to help tell the story. However, long continuous shots do not have to be static as they were in the early films. Film-makers have used them to show off their directorial prowess as seen in *Rope* (1948) where Hitchcock used just nine shots in the whole film, each one carefully choreographed to include depth and movement.

A cutaway is a shot that takes in the surrounding area of the location that is being filmed. As the name suggests it is a general view, rather than of anything specific. Cutaway shots add background and are useful to have during the editing stage. For example, if shooting an interview, the camera is turned around the room and footage is shot of the room in general. These cutaways help give context and add visual interest to the interview.

An insert is a shot that focuses on something specific, so in the interview scenario, for example, the shot could be a close-up on the interviewee's hands, eyes or mouth.

In a scene between two or more people reaction or reverse shots are necessary to cover the action. For example, the camera is pointing at person A to record their dialogue. It is then set up where person A was standing to record person B's response. This gives the impression to the audience that it is involved in the conversation, which can be a more dynamic way of covering the action than having a master shot of both people at the same time.

CREATING A SEQUENCE

Individual shots can be composed in numerous ways and the way in which they are selected, ordered and combined by the director produces different effects.

The director reads each scene and considers the shooting options that will help convey the intended meaning. If the sequence is supposed to create suspense it will be shot differently to how it will be if it is meant to inspire love or hate.

Each individual shot conveys meaning and the combination of shots into a particular order adds further depth. For example, moving from a mid shot to a close-up emphasises the subject and indicates increasing interest. The reverse is signalled by changing the order of the two shots.

A wide, mid and series of close shots are the basics required to cover a scene, which can be added to by as many more shots as time and budget allow.

180 DEGREE RULE OR CROSSING THE LINE

A major consideration in ordering shots is continuity of film space, and a technique known as the **180 degree rule** is usually adhered to in film-making. Whether successive shots will cut together effectively depends on maintaining consistent screen space. There is an imaginary line between two characters in any given scene. Shots can be intercut on the same side of the line, but if the camera crosses that line, film space is ruptured creating a disjointed effect known as a jump cut. This jolts the eye and alerts the audience to the fact that the action is not continuous. Having said this, sometimes film-makers cross the line deliberately to create this effect for stylistic purposes.

1: 180 DEGREE RULE
In the 180 degree rule, the imaginary line between two actors in the same scene should not be crossed.

1: MASTER SHOT
This master shot is used at the beginning of the scene in order to establish the setting and action, before moving into a range of other shots to help tell the story.

2: INSERT
This insert shot moves closer to the action, focusing on the two characters, which involves a close-up of them kissing.

| – Exercise – |

Look at some early single-shot films, such as *The Arrival of a Train at La Ciotat Station* (1896) and *Trip to the Moon* (1902). Make notes on what other shots would be useful to make it more visually interesting and help tell the story.

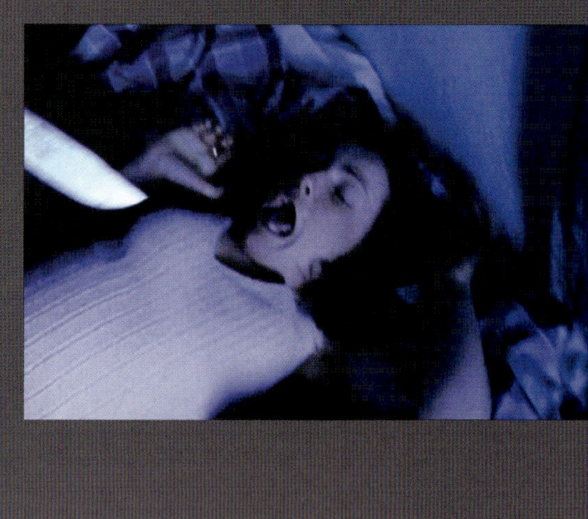

3: CLOSE UP
In this shot the camera is set-up to point at the male character who is talking to the female character.

4: REACTION
In this reaction shot, the camera is set-up to point at the female character in order to record her response to the dialogue. This gives the audience the impression that they are involved in the conversation.

5: MASTER SHOT
In this cutaway shot, the surrounding area of the murder scene is shown giving background information to the audience.

6: INSERT/POINT OF VIEW
This close-up of the knife adds tension to the scene, which is further emphasised by the fact that the audience is seeing it from the point of view of the victim.

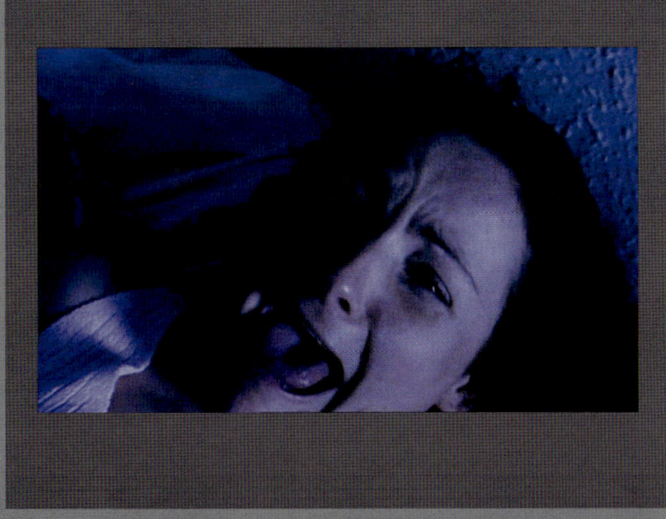

⌃ 7: REACTION
The reaction shot clearly shows the horror in the face of the victim, involving the audience in her terror.

⌃ 8: REVERSE
In this shot the camera points at the face of the murderer.

| – Exercise – |

Watch *No Country for Old Men* (2007) or *There Will Be Blood* (2007) and decide on the order of sequence of shots in the first scene. Why might the director have chosen to film the sequence in this way?

Parallel action

A technique often used in film is parallel action, whereby the shot moves between two events that are happening at the same time. Usually the two scenes being cut between relate to each other, for example, the first scene shows a bank robbery taking place and the second shows the police on their way to the scene. Will the robbers get away with the money? Will the police stop them? It is a useful device in building suspense.

Parallel action can also produce contrast. By showing one scene cut with something completely different both scenes are exaggerated and a sense of difference is promoted. For example, a scene of a huge opulent banquet intercut with a scene of poverty and hardship will accentuate both extremes. Contrast creates drama, which is an essential ingredient in both fiction and documentary production.

1 – 2: **PARALLEL ACTION**
Parallel action builds tension between the two scenes shown, both of which relate to each other.

≈ 3 – 4: PARALLEL ACTION
In these two scenes from *Titanic* (1997) the sinking ship is intercut with Rose being increasingly immersed in water. This creates a sense of tension as the audience is left wondering whether she will escape.
20th Century Fox/The Kobal Collection

The Cattle Trail

Shot List.	Day 1
Location:	Honeydew Farm, Tailor's Lane, Collingbourne-Kingston
Shot 1	L.S of cattle coming from the light outside into the darkness of the milking shed. Tripod. Natural light
Location:	Salisbury Market
Shot 2	C.U of cattle behind bars.
Shot 3	M.C.U of cattle behind bars.
Shot 4	M.S of cattle behind bars.
Shot 5	W.S of cattle walking up ramp into lorry.
Shot 6	W.S cow clambering over another cow.
	All the above handheld
Location:	Fields around Salisbury
Shot 7	L.S. cows in a field.
Shot 8	Medium W.S. 2 or 3 cattle in a field
Shot 9	M.S. of cow turning its head.
	Tripod. Static camera.

1: SHOOTING SCRIPT
A shooting script will be unique to the director who creates it. However, all shooting scripts use the same building blocks.

The **shooting script** is a document that puts all of the shot sequences together. It is the original script with the camera directions added – a paper version of how the director wants the film to be shot. It shows where the camera will be positioned throughout the action and dialogue; whether it will be close-up or far away, and whether it should move slowly following the action or remain static, etc.

Each director will respond differently to a script and produce a unique shooting script, but they will all use the same basic building blocks as discussed previously.

| – Exercise – |

Try writing a shooting script for an idea you have for a script. Try breaking down the same page of script and decide where the camera should be positioned.

Storyboards are drawings of the script, shot by shot, in chronological order. They are a paper version of what will eventually appear on the screen. Each picture illustrates the characters, action and location, accompanied by written information including details such as shot size, camera and character movement, lighting and anything else that helps convey the intention of the shot.

The storyboard helps the director to visualise the script, enabling him or her to clarify ideas and work out certain set-ups of the film in advance of shooting. It can help with the overall structure by identifying areas that are effective and those that may be weaker, thus requiring further work. Storyboards are also a time – and money – saving device. The more preparation carried out during pre-production, the less time will be wasted during production.

Dialogue between the director, director of photography (DOP) and the production designer is facilitated through storyboards. Ideas about the look and style of the film are discussed at this stage. Visual reference material helps convey to everyone working on the film the intentions and ensures a coherent approach, so that everyone is working toward the same goal. Storyboards can help generate the production of drawings of locations, mood boards, scale drawings and 3-D scale models (*see* Chapter 5) created by the art department.

The director talks through each set-up with the DOP in order to clarify issues of camera, lighting, grip equipment (track, crane etc.) and the choice of lenses (*see* Chapter 6).

Storyboards can range from professional artist level to stick men; the level of drafting skill is unimportant. The point is that they must effectively communicate the relevant information for each shot to the team. They are a means to an end – a useful tool – not something to be tortured over in terms of quality of illustration.

The storyboard continues to act as a blueprint and reference throughout production. The film may adapt and grow as new ideas occur, but the storyboard remains a reliable map of the journey through to post-production.

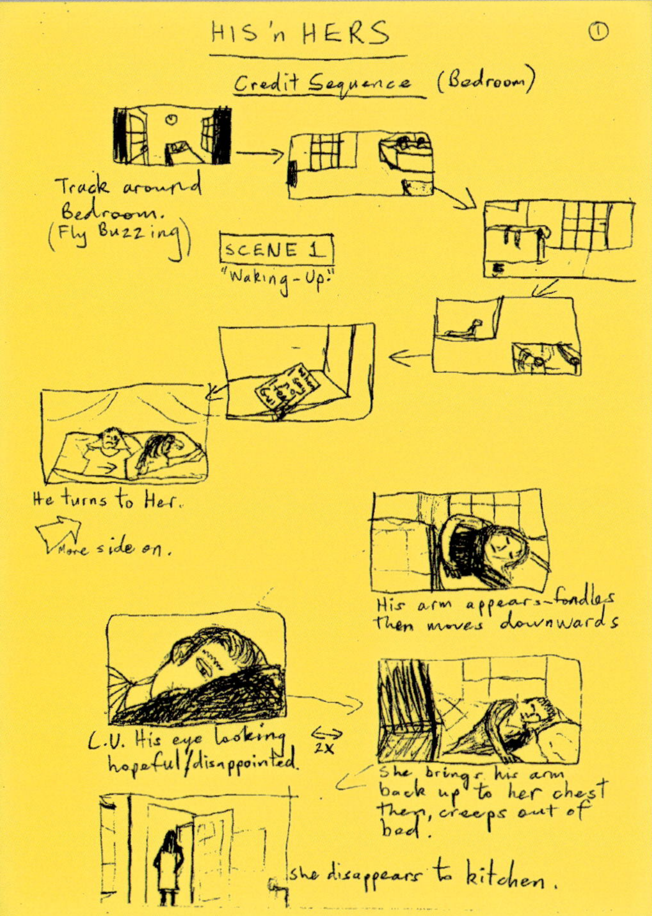

HIS 'n HERS
1
Credit Sequence (Bedroom)
Track around Bedroom. (Fly Buzzing)
SCENE 1
"Waking-Up"
He turns to Her.
More side on.
His arm appears - fondles then moves downwards
C.U. His eye looking hopeful/disappointed.
2X
She brings his arm back up to her chest then, creeps out of bed.
She disappears to kitchen.

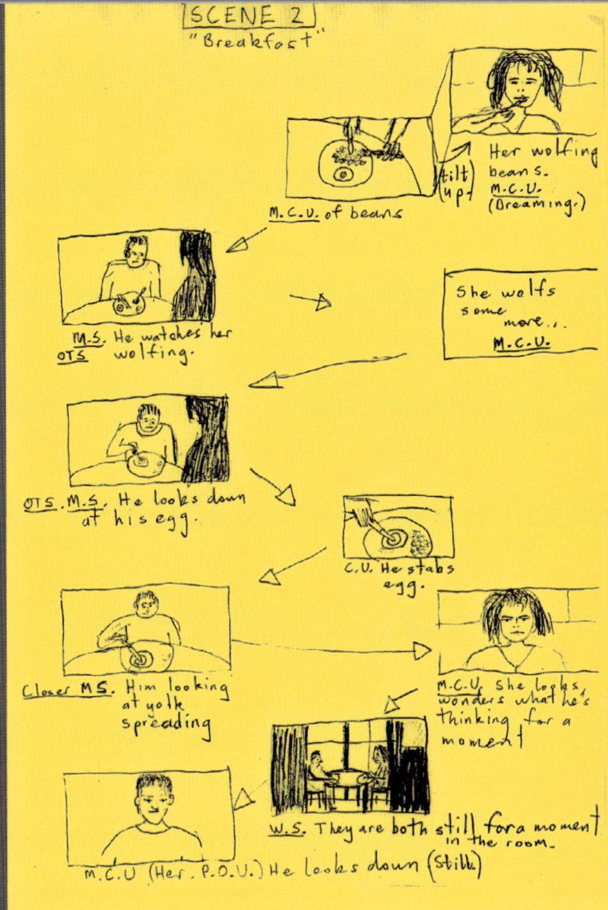

Her wolfing beans. M.C.U. (Dreaming.)

M.C.U. of beans
M.S. He watches her wolfing.

She wolfs some more.. M.C.U.
OTS. M.S. He looks down at his egg.
C.U. He stabs egg.
Closer MS. Him looking at yolk spreading
M.C.U. She looks, wonders what he's thinking for a moment
W.S. They are both still for a moment in the room.
M.C.U (Her. P.O.U.) He looks down (Still)

1 – 2: **STORYBOARDS FROM HIS 'N HERS**
Storyboards do not have to be elaborate as long as they convey the key information required – shot size, framing and composition, camera movement, story, action and sequence.
Director: Campbell Graham

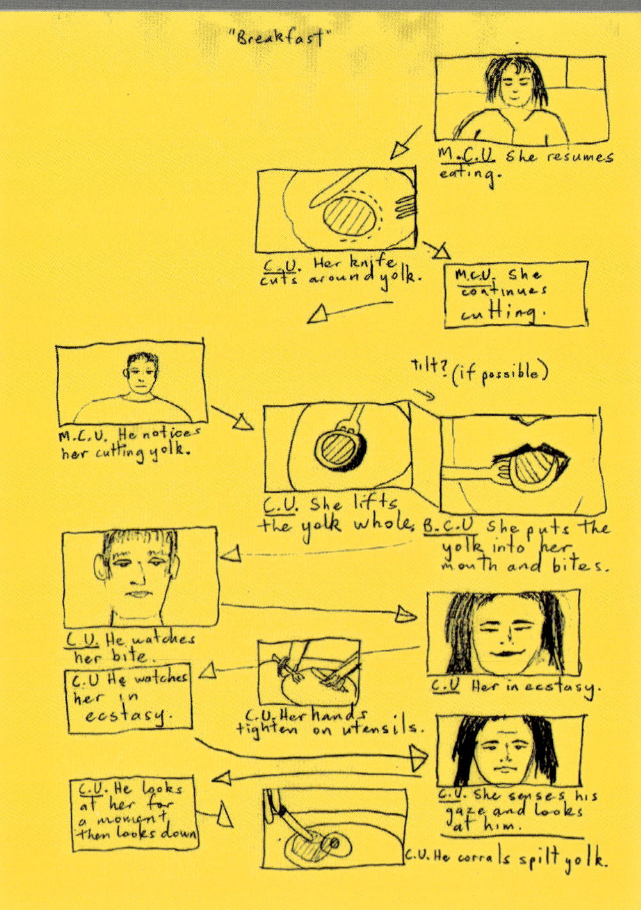

3–6: **STORYBOARDS FROM HIS 'N HERS**
By following the storyboard we can see the scenes of the film unfolding and developing.
Director: Campbell Graham

SCENE 4
"Bus-Stop. 1"
Car wipes screen at start.
L.S. H+H at B/Stop
"I suppose it's that... I never have to do anything...
Track round slowly. Profile → Front
There's always this lump.....
...Nothing would ever happen
C.U. O.T.S Profile
"Yes it would......
"Yes it would....
C.U. O.T.S. Profile
No it wouldn't"
No it wouldn't."
"Well, why don't you just wait a bit and see?"
(It looks like quite a risk.)
Car wipes screen at end.

SCENE 5.
"The Park."
L.S. Coloured kite against blue sky.
M.S. HER serenely flying kite.
"Did you know that women.... Really... Yes."
either
or
grass
(He sidles into frame + out again.
M.S. Downwards.
"It's not healthy, you know...
"Have a wank."
Kite closer
(S.F.X. Flapping increases)
M.C.U.
in
out
"2,000 years ago I'd just have you, you know...etc."
(She turns and looks at him.)
Kite very close
(S.F.X. Loud flapping.)

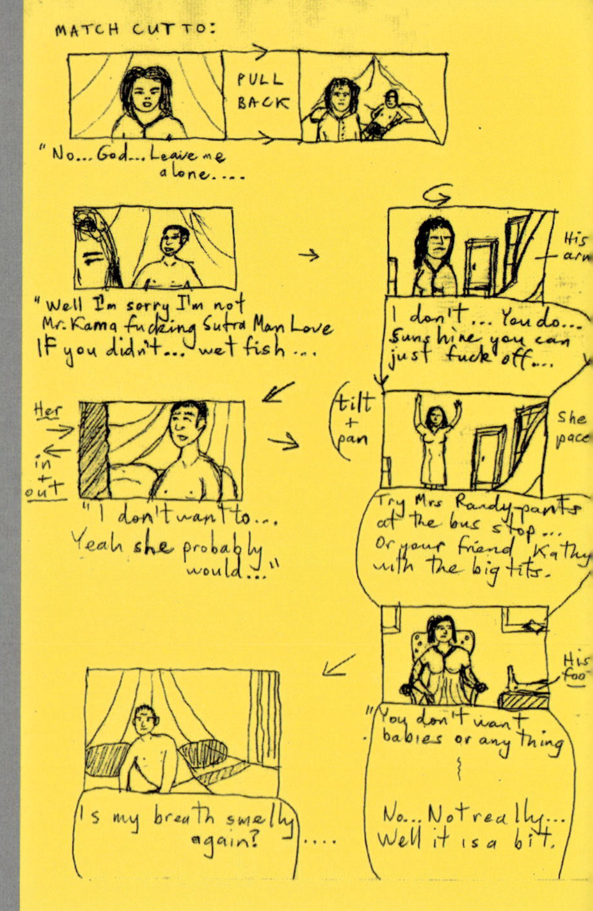

⌃ *7–10:* **STORYBOARDS FROM HIS 'N HERS**
In these storyboards we can see the film climaxing and concluding.
Director: Campbell Graham

Push in
9
feel like some sort of...
"You're not. It's just that I don't feel like it...
Tilt up
Why? etc.
What are you doing?"
Stay somewhere else tonight...
What do you mean?
Handheld?
"I think I'll stay at Sal's." etc
(She leaves to bathroom)
(She collects her stuff.)
New shot
He follows her out of room.

Pan
He searches for trousers and looks out window at her.
1
2.
Pan + tilt to window
"I was so lonely before I met you
Her a bit further
Pan
"Oh... hold on."
(She returns
Pan back
"I shouldn't just be a cure for your loneliness.

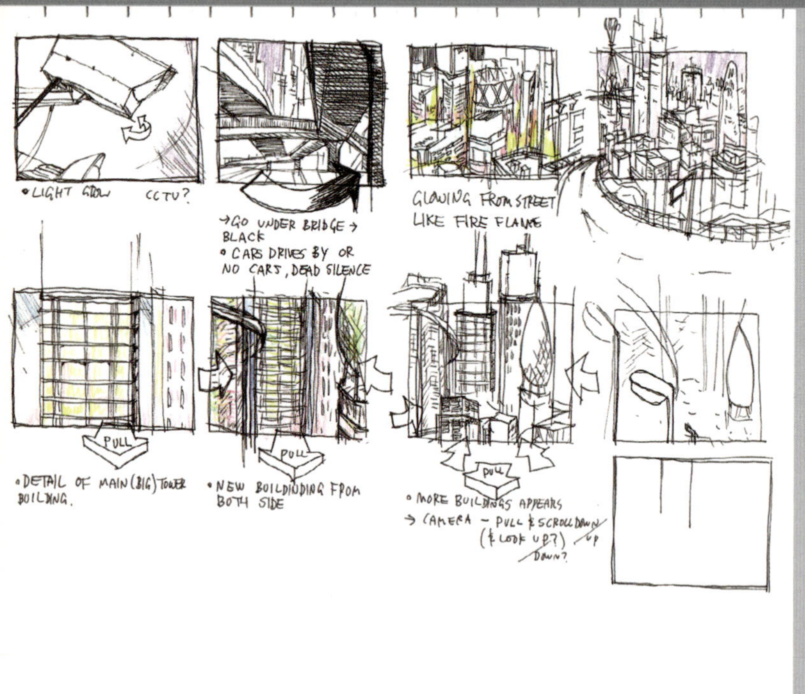

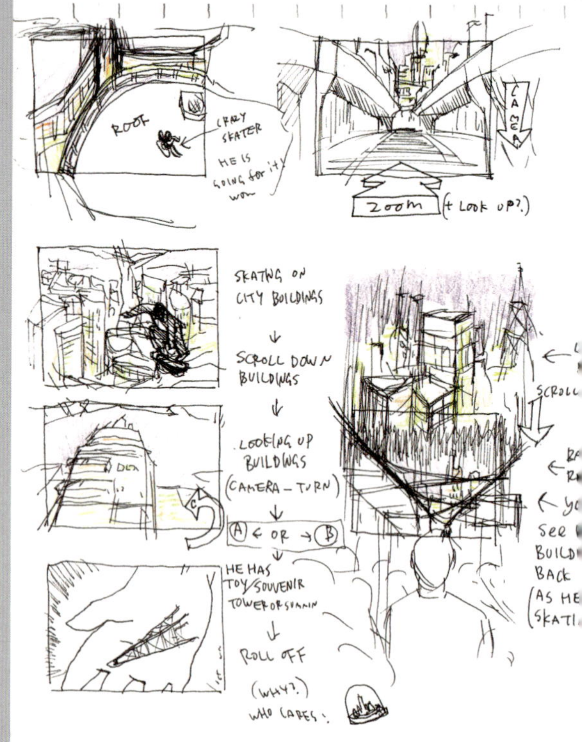

1–4: STORYBOARDS FROM VAUXHALL AD
Storyboards can be very detailed, as those shown here. However, they still convey the same essential material for the direction of the film.
Director: Lucia Helenka

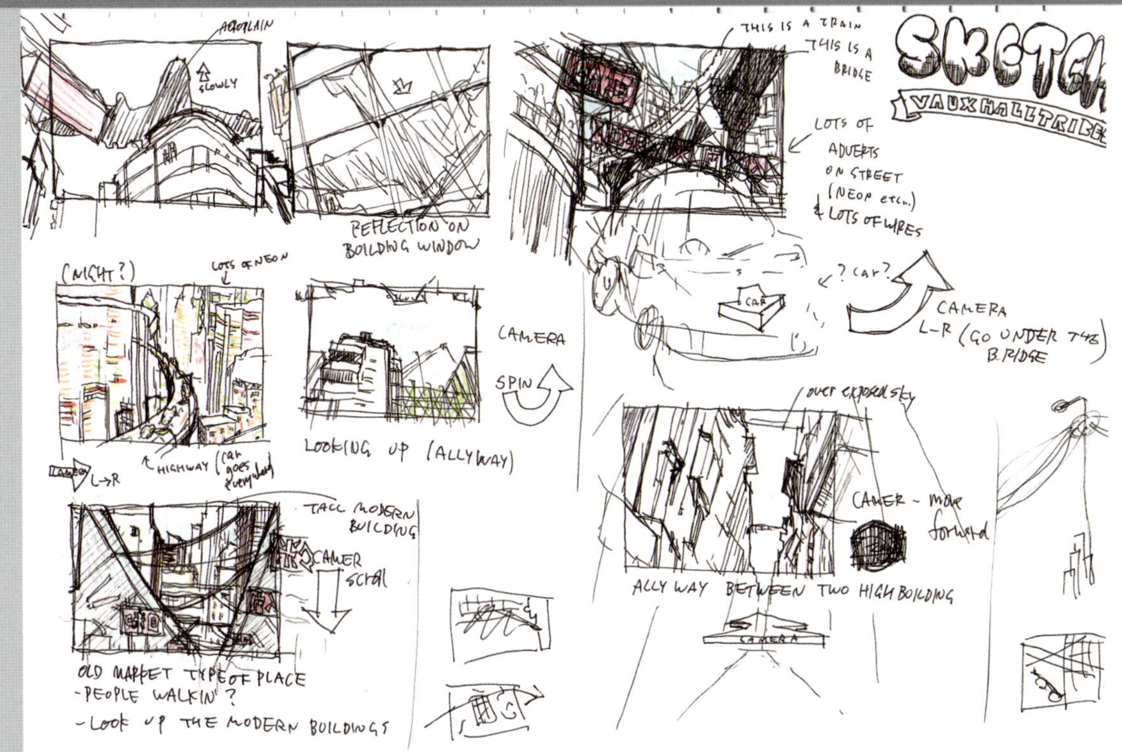
SLOWLY
REFLECTION ON BUILDING WINDOW
THIS IS A TRAIN
THIS IS A BRIDGE
SKETCH
VAUXHALLTRIBE
LOTS OF ADVERTS ON STREET (NEON etc.) & LOTS OF WIRES
(NIGHT?)
LOTS OF NEON
L→R
HIGHWAY
LOOKING UP (ALLYWAY)
CAMERA SPIN
? CAR?
CAR
CAMERA L-R (GO UNDER THE BRIDGE
TALL MODERN BUILDING
ALLY WAY BETWEEN TWO HIGH BUILDING
CAMERA
OLD MARKET TYPE OF PLACE
-PEOPLE WALKIN' ?
-LOOK UP THE MODERN BUILDINGS

Working with actors

Directors don't just direct the camera – they direct the actors too. This usually involves casting, which is where several actors audition for the part. It is a good idea to film the casting so that the performances can be watched back. It is also useful to see how the actors appear on the screen. An actor who is perfect for the stage may not be suitable for film and vice versa, due to the different acting qualities required for each medium. Generally the stage actor uses bigger gestures and projects his or her voice while the screen actor does not need to do this as the camera is close by recording the performance. Some actors have a screen presence and charisma while others don't. Often a director will film the casting as it allows them to see how the actor will appear on camera.

Casting requires a good understanding of who the characters in the script are. This is based on the actor's ability to create a credible persona. How they look is not always as important because appearance can be adapted with costume and make-up.

Once the director has found the cast the rehearsals take place. During the rehearsals the director gets the actors to work through the script, stopping at points to encourage or change the way they are playing the scene. The first rehearsals are usually read-throughs, when the cast go through their dialogue together. The next stage introduces the action, where the actors' movements will be worked out. Depending on the length of the script this process may take days or weeks. The characters will take shape during this period as the actors get to know their parts and understand their motivation (*see* Chapter 2).

« 1: DIRECTION
The director is responsible for rehearsing the actors, taking them through the script and blocking the movement.

The actors block through the movement, which means they work through the scenes and agree where their character will be in the setting throughout. This is a practical necessity and works in conjunction with the final placing of the camera in relation to character positions.

There are a variety of acting approaches and styles. For example, some directors get their cast to improvise rather than work strictly to lines that have been pre-written. Other directors throw the actors into filming without rehearsals because they want the spontaneity that the lack of preparation creates.

1: WORKING WITH ACTORS
The director of photography (DOP) explains how he plans to shoot the scene to the actors.

FAQs

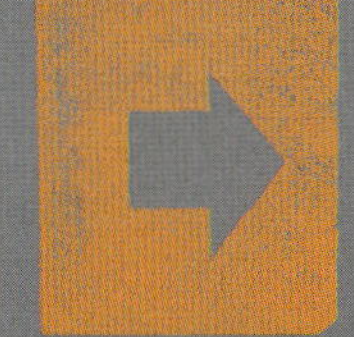

How do I storyboard if I can't draw?
Stick men are fine; the main point is to convey the shot size and movement.

How do I decide which shots to use and in what order?
Watch a lot of films and consider the choices made by different directors.

What if I change my mind – do I have to stick to the shooting script?
The shooting script is an important planning device but shouldn't prevent creativity on the day. As long as you have sufficient time, give it a go.

Where do I find actors for my film?
It depends on the scale of your project. If you are on a limited budget friends are one option. Alternatively, you can post an advert on one of the many websites. There are many actors starting out who will work on a small budget to build up their **showreel**.

Do I have to pay actors?
Again it depends on your budget. You should provide travel and food allowance as a minimum.

Checklist

— Watch lots of films, break them down into the separate shots, and think about why the director has chosen to use them in that way.

— Watch the acting in a diverse range of films from Hollywood to art house. Think about the way the actors play characters and which ones seem more effective to you.

— Practise drawing storyboards and experiment with different approaches.

— Remember that the function of a storyboard is to break the script into its component parts, shot sequences and camera position and movement.

Running glossary

Storyboard – a sequence of drawings representing the frames to be shot for the film

180 degree rule – an imaginary line on one side of the axis of action, e.g. between two actors in a scene. Once established, consecutive shots should remain on the same side of the line and not cross over it

Shooting script – a detailed plan of how each scene will be shot

Showreel – a compilation of previous work to show prospective employers

1: VAUXHALL AD SET
Scale models can be built and used to film on. This can save the time and money that would be involved in building a full-scale construction.
Production designer: Sam Buxton

5 PRODUCTION DESIGN

The production designer is the head of the art department and it is their job to create a **design concept** for the film. This will ultimately define how the whole film looks on-screen. Through the use of space, volume, light, colour and texture, they aim to create a design that supports and strengthens the story and characters.

A designer is required to create film **sets**, buildings, cities or even whole worlds, connecting them to the film's narrative. In a practical sense, they are building somewhere for the action to take place and in a creative sense, making it appropriate for the film and the characters who live there.

The process begins in pre-production with the designer's initial responses to the script in terms of mood, look and technical requirements. The designer must also take into account the characters, the plot and the period that the film is set in. Research is then carried out and from this comes sketches, **technical drawings** and three-dimensional **models** before the final stages of set construction and dressing are carried out.

The script will spark ideas in the designer; they will then begin to consider how to bring these to life in the visual design.

The designer breaks down the script into locations, interiors and exteriors, and day and night time periods. From each of these elements they can see how many settings are required for the film, which could be as few as one to as many as the budget will allow. For each setting another breakdown is produced for all items that appear in the course of the action. In addition to these essential items the designer lists everything else they would like to see in each setting to support the characters and story, such as furnishing and decoration.

SHOOTING SCRIPT
Each set is conceived in relation to the shooting script, which details the camera and actor movements (*see* Chapter 4). The set must be designed appropriately to enable the activity in the shooting script to take place.

BUDGET
The art department receives around 10% of the overall film budget. What eventually appears on the screen is influenced by budgetary constraints; the designer is always looking for ways to stretch and make the most of their resources. Designing relies on the inventive use of the allocated budget as the designer must always contain their ideas within the boundaries of the available time and money. When working with a small budget it can be difficult to meet the requirements of the script, but there are other available options, such as borrowing from shops in return for a credit on the film or buying from antique and vintage shops on the understanding that they will buy back when filming is finished.

SHOOTING SCHEDULE
Keeping up with the schedule is essential so the designer needs to know how long it will take to prepare each set and deploy their team accordingly.

RESEARCH

Decisions about how key settings should look are based on research, which is a fundamental part of the design process. The designer will look at a range of sources that will inform and enrich their work and will help illustrate and embellish the story in the script. Reference material can be varied and is taken from locations, films, paintings, photographs, fashion, textiles and even music.

Research also helps when deciding whether to shoot in a studio or on-location; often a film will combine studio-built sets with existing interior and exterior locations. There are advantages and disadvantages to both studio and location filming. For example, working in a studio means that the environment can be tailored to the script and conditions such as weather will not affect the shoot. On the other hand, working on-location may lend a degree of authenticity. Whether shooting in a studio or on-location, work will need to be carried out to meet the requirements of the script. When shooting on-location, for example, painting and dressing are usually required to adapt the space appropriately (*see* Chapter 3).

Exercise

Look at a script that you have written and make notes on how you might begin to visualise key aspects of the scenes.

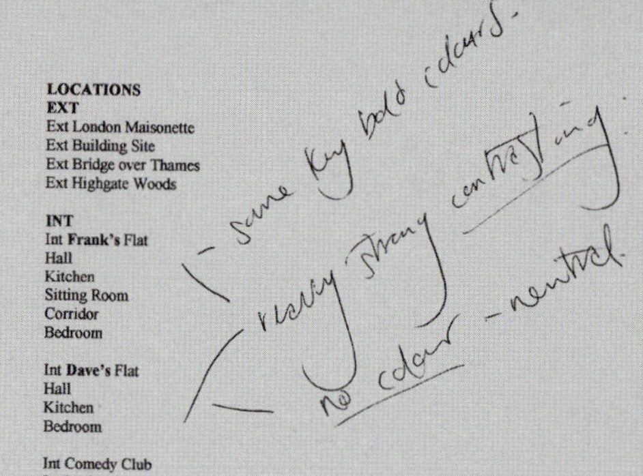
LOCATIONS
EXT
Ext London Maisonette
Ext Building Site
Ext Bridge over Thames
Ext Highgate Woods

INT
Int **Frank's** Flat
Hall
Kitchen
Sitting Room
Corridor
Bedroom

Int **Dave's** Flat
Hall
Kitchen
Bedroom

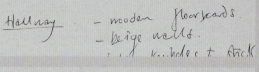

Int Comedy Club
Int Locksmiths shop

1: BREAKING DOWN THE SCRIPT
The script is the starting point for the production designer. The designer breaks down the script into locations, interiors and exteriors, day and night periods. From this they start to research ideas on how to design the settings.

2: RESEARCH
Research is a fundamental part of the production design process. Reference material can be varied and can be taken from a range of sources, including locations, photographs and paintings.

The concept is the unifying principle that creates coherence in the visual identity of the film. Designers may hit on the concept on first reading the script or may need to research different aspects until they uncover something that makes sense. While seemingly intangible, a designer knows when they have found the key to connecting the visuals with the script. Some examples are as follows:

Chinatown (1974) – the absence of water. The designer, Richard Sylbert, used a colour palette that evoked heat: burnt umber to yellow and brown – it is so dry it makes you feel thirsty just watching.

Do the Right Thing (1989) – a desert in the city. This is achieved through the use of colour and a lack of vegetation.

The English Patient (1996) – the contrast between pre-war opulence and post-war austerity. Finding and highlighting a contrast in the drama in this way is a technique used by many designers.

These concepts add depth to the film and operate on a visual and a metaphorical level.

1 – 3: MOOD BOARDS
Mood boards are an important aspect of the creative process. They can include images from magazines, photographs, postcards and fabric – anything that helps to convey the desired look and emotion for the film.
Production designer: Lily Elms

Key questions when considering the spaces and places in which to situate the story are 'Where are we?' and 'Why are we here?'.

Thinking about who the character is and what sort of place they would live or work in is essential. The space defines the character and helps convey ideas about the situation they are in. Size, shape, height, and so on, are essential in designing a space that works with the intentions of the script. For example, a space may be boxed in to signify either poverty or wealth. In *Nil by Mouth* (1997) the council flat is like a fish tank full of people trapped in poverty and crime. In *Match Point* (2005) the wealthy couple are also confined in a glass box, this time reflecting the deceit, adultery and murder of the protagonist.

Space can also be used to promote a contrast, such as in *Closer* (2004), where one couple (Clive Owen and Julia Roberts) live in a spacious artist's loft while the other couple (Jude Law and Natalie Portman) occupy a tiny cramped flat. The former conveys the loneliness and isolation of the couple, the latter the lack of freedom and control.

COMPOSITION

The composition of a scene can comprise of gaps or shadows and is as much about what is left out as what is included in the frame. The formation of shapes such as squares, triangles and circles contribute to the sense of space and are used to convey aspects of the narrative.

⌃ 1: DRESSING ROOM
This scene lacks natural daylight and the eye is drawn to the vanishing point of the triangular composition.
Production designer: Hugo Wyhowski

⌃ 2: THE AVENGERS
In this sketch from *The Avengers* (1998) the ceiling conveys a claustrophobic effect that gives a sense of being trapped.
Production designer: Stuart Craig

| – Exercise – |

Analyse the images above and think about how the composition helps to tell a story or convey a mood.

Decide what direction the light is coming from. Is there one light source or several? What effect does the light have on the scene?

"THE ENGLISH PATIENT"

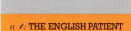

« 1: THE ENGLISH PATIENT
This sketch of Almasy's apartment for *The English Patient* (1996) identifies the space from ceiling height, window and door placement to dressing and props.
Production Designer Stuart Craig

When planning the light for a scene, choices have to be made about its intensity, where it is coming from (direction) and whether it will be natural or artificial (source). If using natural light it can come from windows or doors; if using artificial light it can come from any number of lamps, candles or even a television screen. The DOP and designer work closely on this aspect of the design, coming up with practical and creative solutions (*see* Chapter 6 for further discussion).

The psychological effect of colour can add depth to story and character, so colour choices should be made carefully. For example, red can be used to suggest danger or excitement while black, purple and white are often used for death.

Colour can be used in bold or subtle ways. Designers often shy away from using strong colour in favour of a predominantly neutral palette. When using neutrals, one or two key colours can really stand out for dramatic effect, for example, in *The Ipcress File* (1965), *Schindler's List* (1993) and *Don't Look Now* (1973), red is used to signify danger.

Colour choices can identify characters and places and can be used to highlight difference. For example, in *Shallow Grave* (1994) all of the rooms are based on the colours in Edward Hopper's paintings apart from the room that Keith Allen's character dies in. This marks the room out as different and helps to tell the story.

1: COLOUR PALETTE
The production designer has the whole colour spectrum to choose from and the choices made can influence how the audience experiences mood, atmosphere and emotion in a scene.
Copyright: Vera Bogaerts

⌃ 2 – 3: SHALLOW GRAVE
In this design the colour palette used is based on the paintings of Edward Hopper. The use of purple (a colour often used to symbolise death) in one room makes it stand out from the rest.
Production designer: Kave Quinn

– Exercise –

The Cook, The Thief, His Wife, and Her Lover **(1989),** ***Diva*** **(1981),** ***Edward Scissorhands*** **(1990),** ***Volver*** **(2006),** ***The Wizard of Oz*** **(1939),** ***The Red Shoes*** **(1948). Watch these films and analyse which colours are predominant and which are absent. Think about why those choices have been made and whether you feel they are effective or not. Can you think of other colour choices that would have worked better or helped to tell a different story?**

1: METROPOLIS
Metropolis (1927) is an example of groundbreaking and innovative science fiction design that has been much replicated in later films.
Director: Fritz Lang
UFA / The Kobal Collection

| – Exercise – |
Watch *Metropolis* (1927), *Blade Runner* (1982) and *Children Of Men* (2006). Make notes and think about what visuals are used to construct each of these futuristic landscapes.

When shooting a contemporary film, notions of period are not paramount and as such the designer has fewer restrictions.

If the script is set either in the past or in the future, the designer has to think very carefully about the options available. If the film is set in the past, location shooting will require anything that is not from that period to be removed, such as telegraph poles and yellow lines on roads. Historical research will help inform the designer about how a particular period looked. Watching other films set in the same period will also allow the designer to see how they have been represented. A decision has to be made between strict historical accuracy and conveying the spirit of the time. Often designers prefer the latter as it is less restricting, allowing them to be creative and concentrate on the overall look, rather than on every last historical detail.

When a film is based in the future there are less issues in terms of authenticity because no one knows for sure how the future will look. This allows the designer greater freedom when creating the set.

2: MRS HENDERSON PRESENTS
This set for *Mrs Henderson Presents* (2005), was built at Shepperton Studios to recreate the Soho streets of the war time era.
Production designer: Hugo Wyhowski

1 – 2: SKETCHES
The sketch is the first stage in the design process; it allows the designer to develop their first impressions of the look and feel of the film.
Production designer: Jane Barnwell

The sketch begins the design process; this is then developed further using technical drawings, then scale models and culminates in construction.

SKETCHES

The sketch enables the designer to develop their first ideas and impressions. Sketches can have varying levels of detail and range from a simple line drawing to a full-colour image complete with light sources.

Mood boards are put together using sketches and tear sheets from magazines, all of which help to illustrate the overall design concept and mood. These typically include indications of the stylistic aspects of the design and communicate to the rest of the team the way the designer would like the film to look.

Storyboards are sometimes drawn by the designer, the director, or a separate storyboard artist (*see* Chapter 4).

| – Exercise – |

Try creating a mood board and storyboard a scene from a section of the script from your favourite film.

TECHNICAL DRAWINGS
Architectural drawings are developed for all of the settings that are to be built in the studio. These are to scale and include architectural details such as doors and windows; the dimensions of the set and its contents are also provided on the drawing. Depending on the size of the project either the designer, art director or draftsperson produces the technical drawings and gives them to the construction manager to start building from.

MODELS
A scale model is usually made of the set before it is built. This helps the director and DOP visualise the set as a three-dimensional space, allowing them to discuss potential pitfalls, thus ensuring that they are happy before the set is built.

CONSTRUCTION
The sets are built on sound stages in studios especially designed for film-making. Several sets can be constructed at once which means that while one set is shot on, another can be dressed or built. The varying stages of completion will be scheduled in accordance with the shooting script.

1: MODELS
A scale model of the set is usually made before it is built. This is important as it ensures that the everyone is happy with the design before money and time are spent on the construction.
Production designer: Sam Buxton

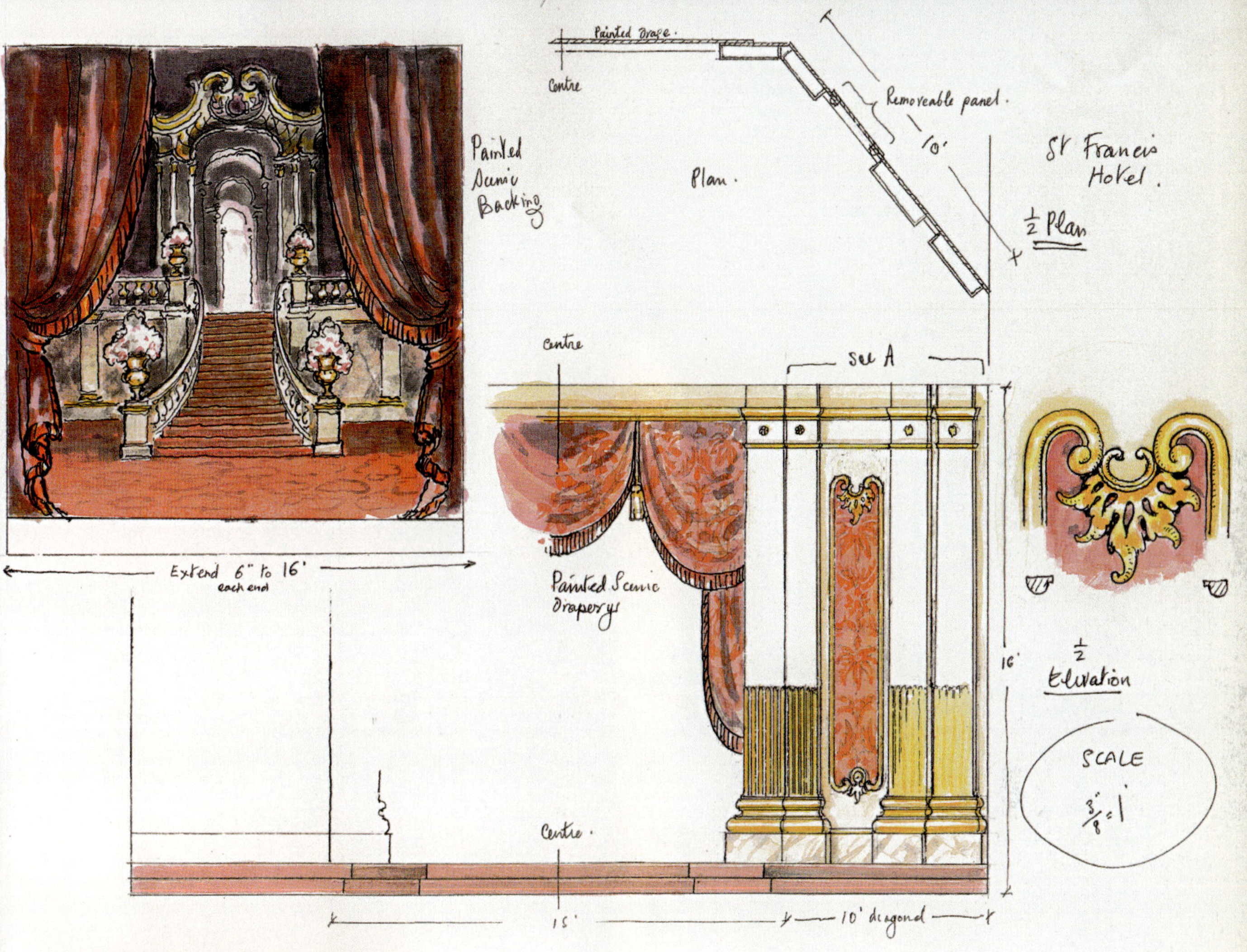

^ 2: **VELVET GOLDMINE**
This illustration is a scale drawing of a portion of the set that was to be built for *Velvet Goldmine* (1998).
Production designer: Christopher Hobbs

SET DRESSING

Once the set is built, the **set dressing** takes place, whereby the set is decorated and dressed with items including furnishings, drapes and **props**. Props can add authenticity to a film and help to bring a space to life.

There are prop houses that hire a huge selection of objects for use in films. However, prop hire can be expensive and as a result low-budget films often rely on borrowing items from shops in return for credit on the film. Another solution is to buy from second-hand shops.

⌃ 1 – 2: DIRTY PRETTY THINGS
This corridor from the set of *Dirty Pretty Things* (2002) shows the evolution that takes place during the process of building and dressing a set.
Production designer: Hugo Wyhowski

3: PROPS
Props are an important aspect of the set dressing. They can add authenticity to a film and can bring a space to life.

Special effects

A special effect is an image created by technical means. There are two different types of special effect; visual effects that use special photographic processes (created in-camera), and mechanical or optical effects that are created in front of the camera.

Special effects have been used on the screen since the beginning of cinema. Traditional effects include painted backdrops, scale models, glass shots, matte shots and rear and front projection.

There are various techniques used to deal with complex special effects that can save both time and money. For example, a three-dimensional model can be built of the setting, which is then filmed. This technique was employed in the futuristic cityscapes of *Metropolis* (1927) and *Blade Runner* (1982).

Another helpful device when creating settings is the use of paintings. Scenery is often created using a painted backcloth that depicts a landscape or cityscape.

More recently, the ability to digitally manipulate images during post-production has opened up new possibilities, as demonstrated in films like *Sin City* (2005), where the entire setting has been computer generated through the use of **CGI** (computer-generated imagery).

PRODUCTION

Depending on the size of the project the designer may or may not be present during shooting. On larger projects there is usually an on-set art director who ensures the designer's wishes are communicated. It is also important to have someone following the continuity of setting and props so that items do not appear or disappear mysteriously from one frame to the next. Action props like candles that can burn down or food and drink that can appear at different stages of consumption need to be monitored carefully.

POST-PRODUCTION

During editing unwanted footage is discarded, which can mean losing a lot of what the designer has created. This could be a wide shot, a small detail or an entire set. Designers accept that this is a necessary part of the job of supporting and embellishing the story and characters – not about their design in isolation – so if it doesn't contribute it has to go.

1: SPECIAL EFFECTS
Special effects help to add drama and action to a scene, whether they are created in-camera or in front of the camera.
Copyright: Lars Christensen

2: THE AVENGERS
In this illustration from The Avengers (1998) the designer has considered the use of special effects for the tornado, which will be added in post-production.
Production designer: Stuart Craig

A character, film or genre can be defined by the costume; think of Dorothy's red shoes in *The Wizard of Oz* (1939); Indiana Jones's safari gear, hat and bullwhip; the shiny black bodysuit of Edward Scissorhands; or the trilby hat worn by all film noir detectives.

The designer works closely with the costume designer to ensure the setting and the costumes tie together in terms of look and mood. If there is a specific colour palette being used then the costume and the settings should be consistent with this. The clothes a character wears provide a lot of information, from personality to financial situation. Again, research is essential in achieving a wardrobe that supports the personality and situation of each character in the film.

A breakdown of the script is necessary to see which different scenes each actor appears in, and to ascertain how many costume changes or adjustments are needed for each. The continuity of this breakdown must be followed closely to avoid inconsistencies such as a character wearing a tie one minute and not the next, or more drastically, a completely different outfit.

On a big-budget film lavish designs may be possible. On the opposite scale, actors in low-budget films may be required to bring suitable items from their own wardrobes.

1: COSTUME
The choice of costumes is essential in order to create credible characters.
Copyright: Ljupco Smokovski

FAQs

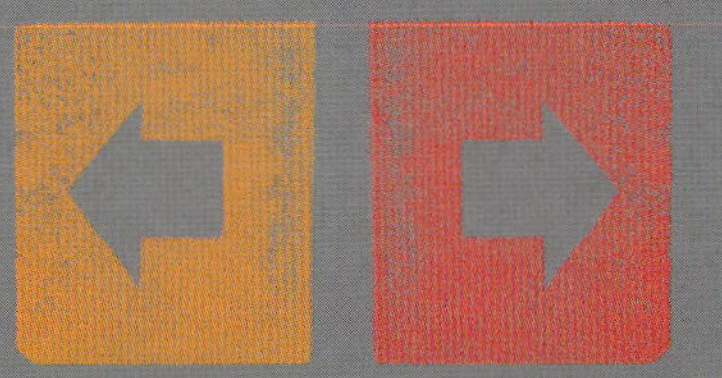

How do you come up with a concept?
There is no sure way of doing this, but reading the script and thinking about key ideas in it that jump out can produce results. Many designers look at paintings or still photography for inspiration.

Is it better to build a set or use an existing location?
It depends on the script and the sort of setting you are trying to create. A built set can be tailor-made while an existing location must be adapted to your needs.

How can I learn about shot composition?
By analysing film design and breaking down what has been positioned in the frame and to what effect. Practising composing your own shots with a stills camera can help you think about the frame.

How do I decide on a colour palette for my film?
It should usually be driven from the script. So, for example, *Dick Tracy* (1990) uses flat cartoon primary colours because it is based on a comic strip, and *Chinatown* (1974) uses brown, parched-earth tones because it is about the absence of water.

- During pre-production the designer conceptualises, researches, draws, plans and builds the settings for the film.
- The original idea has to be workable within the parameters of the production, which means feasible on the time and money available.
- Decide on light source, intensity and direction for each setting.
- Consider what sort of size space will be most effective for the aims of the story.
- Make sketches and mood boards to convey ideas to the rest of the team.
- Research character, place and period (if the film is not contemporary).

Running glossary

Design concept – the idea that gives the film a coherent look

Set – a place or space used for shooting a scene in

Technical drawings – the architectural drawings of sets to be built and constructed

Model – a small-scale building of the set to be constructed which is used for planning purposes during pre-production

Set dressing – the arranging of the furnishing in the set according to the designer's plan

Props – the furniture and objects to be used on-set

CGI – computer-generated imagery – using digital software to create or enhance a scene

1: CINEMATOGRAPHY
Cinematography is created through the positioning of the camera and the choices of lenses, film stock and lighting. It can be expressive and evocative, creating impressive effects.

6 CINEMATOGRAPHY

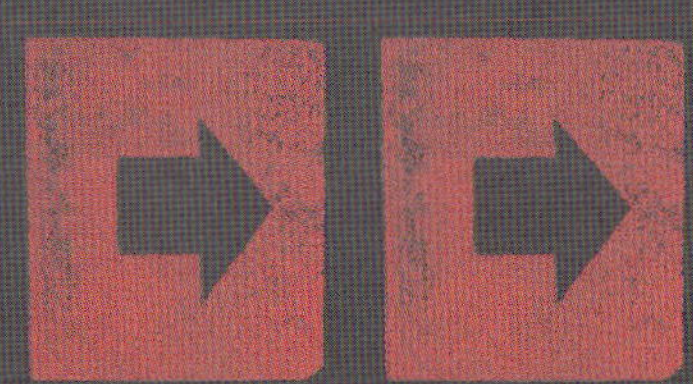

The cinematographer or director of photography (DOP) is the person who makes the director's vision a reality, through the positioning of the camera and choice of lenses, film stock and lighting. The DOP creates mood and emotion through the use of light, shade and composition. On a large-scale production the DOP may not operate the camera but will ensure all of the technical and practical elements are in place ready for shooting.

For each scene they may shoot at least three different set-ups or angles with different focal lengths, camera positions and types of camera movement. There are usually several takes of each to try and capture the best one for technical and performance purposes. On most films there is a shooting ratio that relates to how much more film is shot compared to the duration of the finished film. On a big-budget film hours and hours of footage are shot and only a small proportion of this will make it to the screen.

This chapter introduces the technical, practical and creative fundamentals involved in the cinematography of the film.

The number of formats can be confusing but, essentially, moving images come from either a film or digital video camera. Within this distinction there is a further division between what is known as domestic and professional quality. With digital video, for example, MiniDV is for domestic use while DVCAM and HD (high definition) cameras are for professional use, providing clearer, sharper pictures. Mainstream feature films are usually shot on 35mm film while documentaries tend to use digital formats, which is the more economical option. (*See* Chapter 3 for information on the different film and tape stocks to consider.)

When shooting on film there is a diverse choice of stock, all of which responds differently to light. Film stocks differ in several ways, including where they should be used (either inside with tungsten light or outside with daylight), speed (high, medium and low), size (Super 8, 16mm or 35mm) and how they reproduce colour. It can cost hundreds of pounds to buy a reel of film that will last six minutes. Typically the DOP will test different stock to find the one that creates the effect they would like for each particular scene. In some cases digital and film formats are combined to interesting effect.

FILM LOADING

On digital formats the tape is inserted into the camera ready for recording. Colour bars are the vertical lines recorded at the start of a new tape. This is a convention that helps to create smooth recording. Colour bars are also used to line up the editing so that there is consistency of colour. From the left of the screen the order of colour is: white, yellow, cyan, green, magenta, red, blue and black.

Film loading is a skilled process, whereby the unexposed film spool is transferred from the can to the film magazine in a special black bag to avoid light exposure. The camera assistant is trained to load the film without being able to actually see into the sealed loading bag.

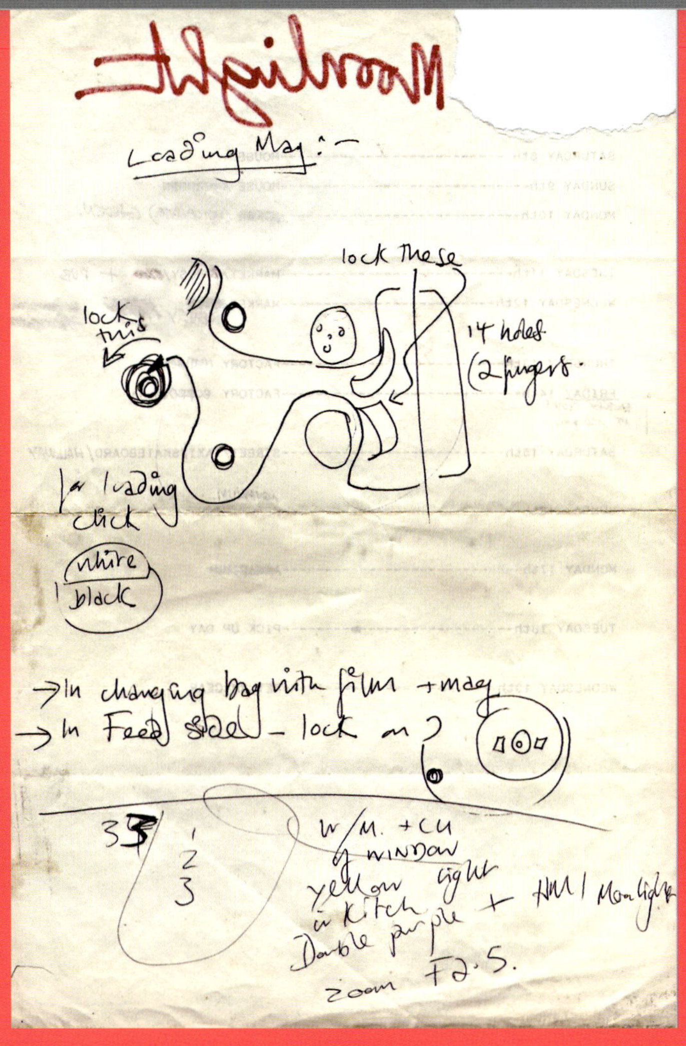

LOADING the Magazine
The Westall WAY...

LABEL FOR FEEDSIDE →
① STOCK TYPE (ie. 7248)
② BATCH NO (BENEATH ie. 022 150.2)
③ Length loaded (
④ date loaded.
⑤ who loaded.
⑥ DIRECTOR. (DIR ...)
⑦ CAM ...
⑧ MAG. NO. (ie 1, 2 or 3).
⑨ PROD.
⑩ NSFTV.
EXPOSED
all info on other side
except footage leave blank
(++.....)

⌃ 1 – 2: LOADING A FILM
Loading the film magazine is a skilled process and is one that requires training.

1: CAMERA MOVEMENT AND MOUNTING
The tripod and the camera crane are two of the most fundamental pieces of equipment to the cinematographer. Both ensure smooth and steady filming.

2: CRANE ARM
There are a range of mountings available for the camera. One example is a crane arm, suitable for making the most of shooting in areas that are restricted in terms of space.

CAMERA MOUNTINGS

There are a variety of mountings for the camera that enable smooth and steady filming. The most fundamental of these is the tripod, which provides a steady platform for static shots and the controlled movement of the camera from a fixed position. The height can be adjusted and a spirit level is included to help ensure the camera is not mounted at an angle. Dolly, track, Steadicam and crane are other options that offer more complex and sophisticated movement.

RECORDING

When filming, light enters the camera through the lens and is focused on to a strip of celluloid coated in chemicals. The chemicals react to the light and form an image, which appears when developed. The film camera records 24 frames a second.

The clapperboard is used to mark the beginning of each take recorded so that the take can be identified later during the editing stage. Scene information is written on the board; this includes the take number, which is the number spoken while the board is clapped in shot so that picture and sound can be synchronised.

Time code is recorded on digital tape and enables the operator (and later the editor) to identify the footage by a series of numbers indicating the hours, minutes, seconds and frames that have passed.

When going for a take, there is a standard procedure to follow:

— 1st Assistant
'Quiet on set please. Going for a take'

— Camera operator
'Board in please'
(Camera assistant puts board in shot)

— Director
'Turn over'

— Camera operator
'Rolling'

— Sound recordist
'Speed'

— Camera operator
'Mark it'

— Camera assistant
'Scene no . . . shot no . . . take no . . .'
Claps board.

— Director
'Action'

— Director
'Cut'

At the end of the take the camera operator checks the 'gate' (camera lens) is clean. If it isn't clean they call 'hair in the gate', a term used for the presence of any dirt or foreign object. Another take will then be necessary.

On digital formats the operator may check at this time that the footage has recorded.

The DOP works closely with the director to compose the images for the film. For each shot they plan what distance, angle and lens will be most effective. The viewfinder on a camera indicates the edges of frame to the operator. It is also useful to have a separate monitor which the director and other crew can view during filming.

There are differences between the way the human eye and the camera see. We have two eyes, which results in our three-dimensional vision. In order to create the illusion of depth for the two-dimensional world of film, light is used. So, although the screen is flat and the film image is a two-dimensional representation of a three-dimensional world, the impression of depth is created through lighting, focus and tone.

^ 1: LOOKING ROOM
In this shot from *Him Over There*, the brick wall provides a geometric backdrop and the space created allows the subject to look across frame.
Student film-maker: John Vanderpuije

Picture composition and framing

In composing the frame the DOP is actively making choices about what is included in the image in terms of stylistic and narrative conventions. Each shot conveys information to the audience, which exacts an intended reaction. What is left out of the frame is as important as what is put in. For example, framing usually allows for **headroom**, which is space above the subject so they do not appear too tightly cropped. **Looking room** is another deliberate space in the composition, which allows the subject to look across frame.

Space is organised to avoid positioning the subject centre screen as this can create a flat effect lacking visual interest. A more effective composition can be achieved by dividing the screen into thirds vertically and horizontally and putting subjects on these lines or where they intersect (fifths and eighths are also used in this way). This is known as the rule of thirds.

2: HEADROOM
In this shot from *Him Over There* the headroom and vertical lines in the shot create an interesting pattern for the composition.
Student film-maker: John Vanderpuije

Lines, shape, form, texture and pattern are used to convey meaning in the frame. Compositional lines can be created through nature (for example a tree) or can be man-made (for example a lamp post) – the thicker the line the stronger the message. Lines can join to create shapes, such as squares and circles; for example, a block of flats is a rectangle and the sun is a circle. While a shape is two-dimensional, form is three-dimensional, thus amplifying the message. Form is created through light and shadow to give the impression of depth, so a circle becomes a sphere, a square a cube and so on. Textures add further depth to the composition with soft, smooth and silky ones being more attractive to us than rough, jagged harsh surfaces. Lighting is used to help exaggerate an uneven surface or bleach out and flatten it. When lines, shapes, forms or textures are repeated at intervals a pattern effect is created.

1: URBAN SETTING
The composition, framing and lighting in this shot from *Roll Deeper* (2006) combine to produce a night-time urban setting.
Director: Lucia Helenka

An outline of lines and their significance is as follows:

— VERTICAL
formality, height, restriction, pride, dignity

— HORIZONTAL
openness, restfulness, tranquillity

— DIAGONAL
dynamism, vibrancy

— CURVED
beauty, elegance, gentleness

An outline of shapes and their significance is as follows:

— SQUARE/RECTANGLE
stability, man-made world

— PYRAMID/TRIANGLE
balance, endurance

— CIRCLES
universality, warmth, wholeness, centrality

— SILHOUETTES
strength

| – Exercise – |
Visit an art gallery or consult art books; look for compositional lines and shapes in the frames and sketch one example of each.

⌃ 1: COMPOSITIONAL LINES
Compositional lines can be natural or man-made. Here the lines of the telegraph pole create a visual pattern in the frame.

« 2: COMPOSITIONAL SHAPES
In this scene from *Once Upon a Time in the West* (1968) a triangle-shape frame is created for the character by shooting through the legs.
Director: Sergio Leone
Paramount/The Kobal Collection

Lighting

Lighting conveys mood and helps the audience understand elements within the scene, creating a sense of place, time, weather and even state of mind. Lighting effects are achieved through a variety of techniques created by the positioning, direction and quality of different types of light.

The lighting style is discussed with the DOP, the director and the production designer, all of whom agree on an approach based on the setting and mood of the film. Learning about how to manipulate light is fundamental to the DOP. 'Painting with light', as it is sometimes called, is a highly creative skill that takes time to master. Light and shadow are essential to create contrast; without either the frame would be flat.

Setting the lights ready for action can be very time-consuming. A lot of elements need to be taken into consideration, such as the camera position and movement, the setting and the actor positions. The entire scene is not usually lit consistently (unless it is a daytime TV show); instead certain objects or spaces are highlighted over others, drawing attention to desired points. As soon as a light is introduced a shadow is cast as a result. Some of these shadows are appropriate and helpful to the scene while others, such as a sound boom or camera, are not.

Light can be measured using a light meter, which is useful in maintaining consistency during a scene. It also enables correct exposure and aperture settings (*see* lenses, page 148). The illumination of light falling on a subject is measured in foot candles – one foot candle is the amount of illumination produced by a single candle at a distance of one foot away from the subject. A lux is the European equivalent of a foot candle; one square meter per single candle (digital cameras measure light in lux).

Lighting quality refers to the light intensity. Hard light (from a small and intense light source) creates crisp, clear images with bold and clearly defined shadows. Soft light (from a large and diffuse source) creates diffused, softer images with less contrast between light and shade. Lights can be flagged or softened with trace or scrim to diffuse them, or bounced using reflector boards or walls – all of which helps to soften the effect.

1: LOW-KEY LIGHTING
Venetian blinds are used in this scene from *Making a Killing* (2002) to break-up the light and to create low-key lighting.
Director: Ryan L. Driscoll

2: PYSCHO
In this scene from *Psycho* (1960) the venetian blinds cast shadows and create patterns across the characters.
Director: Alfred Hitchcock
Paramount/The Kobal Collection

TYPES OF LIGHTS

Lights have spot and flood facilities to provide hard or soft light and adjustable barn doors to shape the beam of light. There are specialist companies that hire lights, filters and accessories to cater for film-making.

Lighting direction refers to the direction from which the light travels to the subject being lit. Front lighting is lighting from the front, which usually eradicates shadows – it can also make the image appear flat. Back lighting is light directed from behind, which defines depth in the image by distinguishing between the subject and the background. Often this creates a rim of light around the edges of the subject, which can result in a silhouette. Side lighting is light directed from the side – it sculpts the shape and texture of the subject and casts strong shadows. Under lighting is light from below, which can distort the appearance of the subject because it tends to look unnatural due to the fact that our natural light comes from above from the sun. This technique is often used to disorientate or disturb the viewer and is frequently seen in horror films. Top lighting is lighting from above, which gives a concentrated spotlight effect.

The use of only one light source is a rarity, but when it is used it creates a dramatic effect with strong shadows and silhouettes. It is more common to use a number of light sources to create a more balanced image.

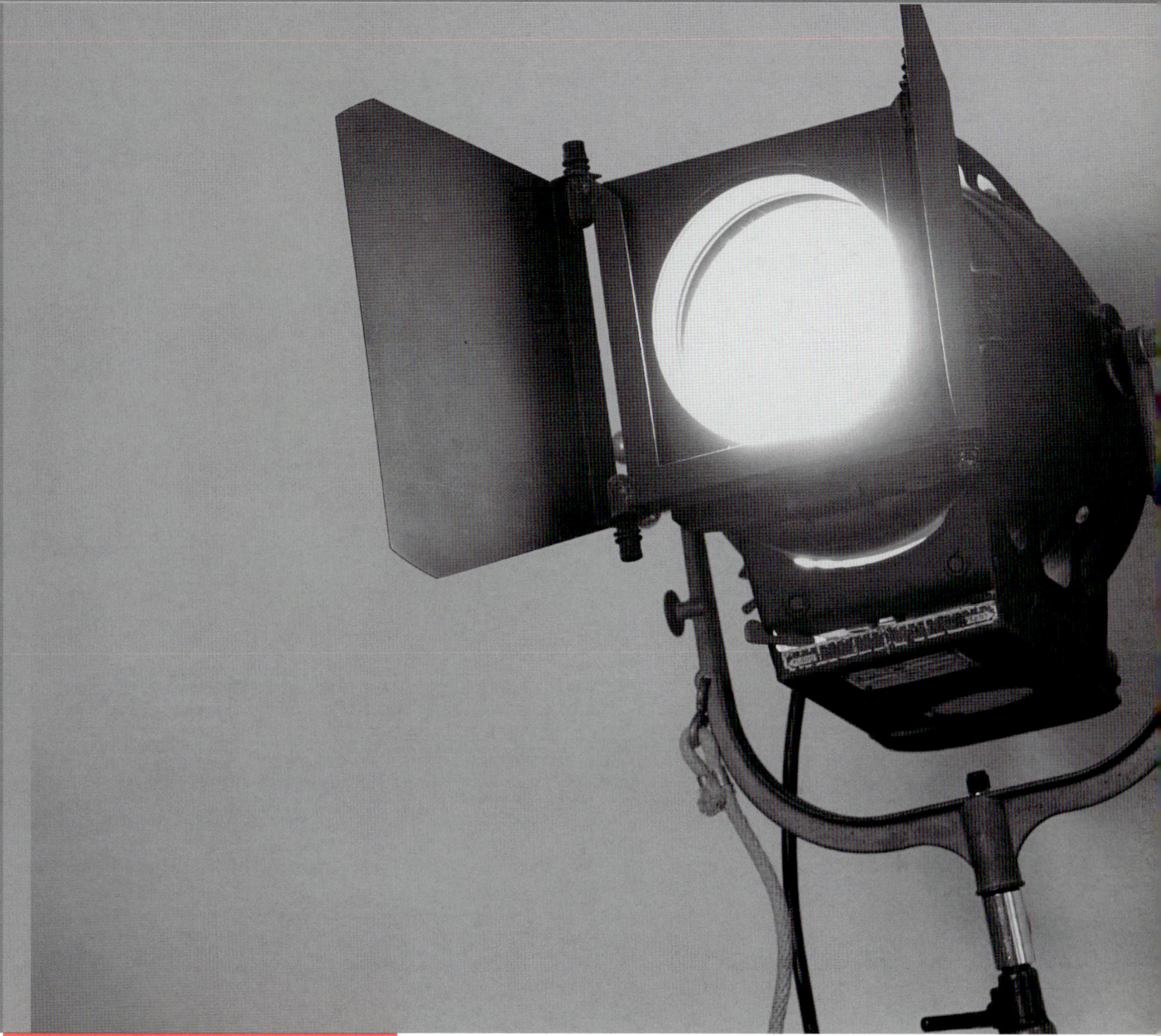

1: LIGHTING
There are a vast range of lights available to the film-maker. Each will create a different mood and atmosphere when used appropriately.
Copyright: Digitalskillet

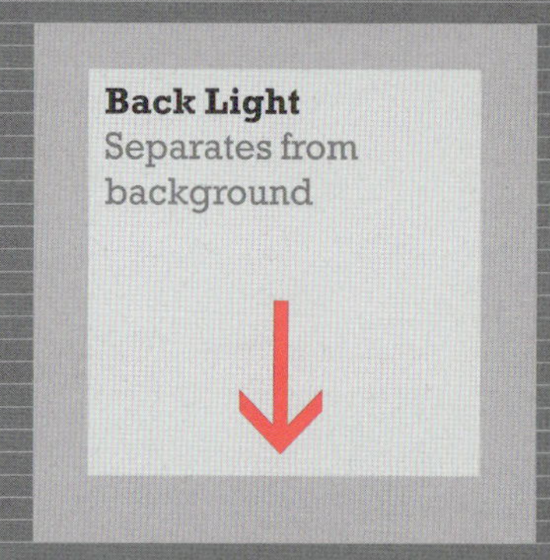

1: THREE POINT LIGHT
Three point lighting is the term used to refer to a basic lighting design using three lights. This consists of the key light, back light and fill light.

Three point lighting is a basic lighting design using three lights. The main source is designed to originate from elements such as windows or lamps, for example, and is the brightest light and therefore casts the greatest shadow. The distinction should be made here between what are known as the practical lights and the film lighting. The practical lights are those appearing in the shot (domestic lights, such as a table lamp) used as the motivation for the film lights, which do not usually appear on-screen.

The back light creates a rim around the subject separating them from the background and adding depth to the image. This is usually positioned above and behind the subject and often points toward the camera, making it necessary to employ flags to prevent glare.

The key light is the brightest light source, intended as the dominant light in a scene, for example the sun or interior artificial lighting, and sets the major colour temperature for the scene. The angle and position of the key light is usually decided by the DOP. Some sources recommend that it should be set at 45 degrees above the camera and from 60 to 40 degrees to one side of the camera.

1: LOW-LIT SCENE
In this shot from *Roll Deeper* (2006) lighting has been employed in a way that illuminates the character's face whilst maintaining the rest of the scene in shadow.
Director: Lucia Helenka

2: WELL-LIT SCENE
This shot from *Roll Deeper* (2006) uses natural daylight to illuminate the scene.
Director: Lucia Helenka

1: LOW-KEY LIGHTING
Low-key lighting, as used in this studio interior, creates contrast through the use of shadow.

2: HIGH-KEY LIGHTING
High-key lighting is bright and energetic and tends to convey a sense of realism. It is often used in studio-based productions.

3: TOP LIGHTING
Top lighting is lighting from above. It is used to give a concentrated spotlight effect, as in this still from *Roll Deeper* (2006).
Director: Lucia Helenka

The fill light is used to soften the shadows created by the key light and to reduce contrast. It is usually a softer, more diffuse light, such as reflected light from clouds or buildings.

Two distinctive styles of lighting are high-key and low-key. Low-key lighting uses only the key and back light, thus sharp contrasts of light and shade are created. This lighting is dark and dramatic and is prevalent in film noir and horror films. High-key lighting employs a lot of fill light, which makes the image softer and less dramatic/expressionistic, but more realistic. This style is bright and energetic and is frequently used in comedies and magazine formats.

| – *Exercise* – |

Analyse the stills featured in this chapter and think about where the main light source is coming from and what effect it has on the scene.

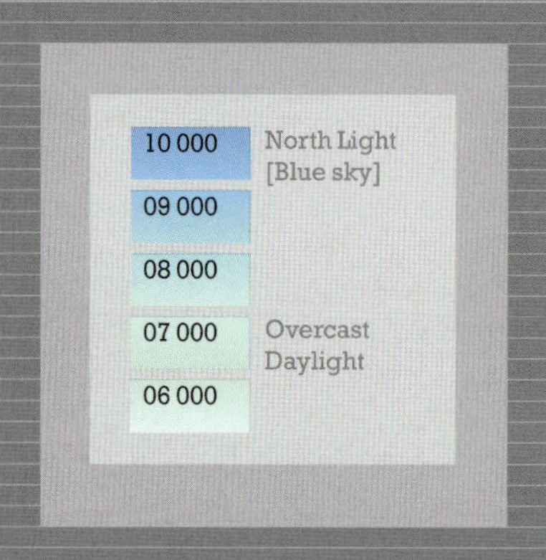

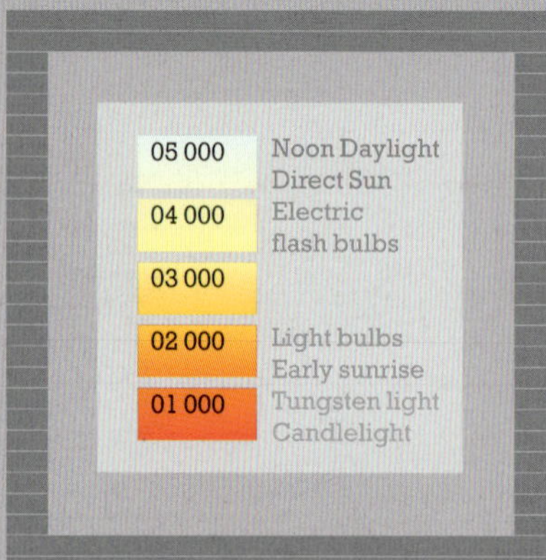

White light is made up of the colours of the visible spectrum, which are red, orange, yellow, green, blue and violet. We interpret surfaces around us as different colours depending on what range of the spectrum they reflect. Different light radiates different intensities known as colour temperature, which is measured in kelvins (after Lord Kelvin who discovered the system). Warmer colours such as red have a lower kelvin rating than cold colours such as blue; so the higher the temperature in degrees kelvin the cooler the colour. If light sources are mixed, correction filters can work to balance the light, for example, blue filters convert tungsten to daylight (on lights) and orange filters convert daylight to tungsten (on windows).

The colour temperatures for daylight, interior light and fluorescent light are as follows:

— Daylight (blue colour temperature) = 5600 degrees kelvin (varies according to weather conditions)

— Interiors (orange/yellow) = 3200 degrees kelvin

— Fluorescent light = 4800 degrees kelvin

1: COLOUR TEMPERATURES
The colour temperatures for daylight, interior light and fluorescent light differ and it is important that the cinematographer is aware of these so that the correct lighting for each scene can be chosen.

The colour of the light as it appears in the scene can be altered by placing transparent coloured filters in front of the lights. This means that the DOP can cast any colour light into the shot to create a natural or artificial effect, from subtle straws to shocking pinks.

A list of colour definitions:

— HUE
The predominant sensation of colour – red, blue, etc.

— PRIMARY COLOURS
Two colours that when mixed produce other colours of the spectrum (for light: red, green and blue)

— COMPLEMENTARY COLOURS
Two colours which when combined produce white light (e.g. blue and yellow) or in pigments to produce black

— SHADE
A hue mixed with black

— TINT
A hue diluted with white

WHITE BALANCE

White balance is the procedure used to ensure that a digital camera is combining the three primary colours in the correct proportions to ensure a balanced picture. This procedure is carried out in the intended light conditions of the shoot.

1: ADDITIVE AND SUBTRACTIVE COLOUR
The additive colour system is the system that mixes red, green and blue to make all other colours. The subtractive colour system is the system that mixes cyan, yellow and magenta to make all other colours.

There are different lenses for different situations and the skilled DOP knows when to use a lens for a particular effect in order to benefit the film.

FOCAL LENGTH

The first consideration when thinking about focal length is to decide how much of the image should be in sharp focus. There is a choice between a lens with a fixed focal length, known as a 'prime lens', and a variable length, known as a 'zoom lens'. A zoom has a continuous focal length over a specified range, so it can be adjusted, making it suitable for general purpose. Prime lenses tend to be used more professionally because they have larger apertures and need less light than a zoom.

The amount of a scene that will appear in the picture will depend on the lens angle. A wide-angle lens has a short focal length, which gives a wide-angle view. A telephoto lens, on the other hand, has a long focal length, which produces a narrow angle allowing it to see objects in the distance as being close-up.

APERTURE

The iris or aperture is the hole through which light is admitted through the lens. The larger the aperture the more light that enters and the brighter the image is as a result. Consequently the aperture affects the picture exposure and **depth of field** in which subjects appear in focus. Lenses can be stopped down to limit the amount of light or opened up to allow more light in. When the image is underexposed the lens aperture can be increased or additional lighting can be used to produce a more balanced picture. If overexposure is the problem then aperture and/or lighting can be decreased.

DEPTH OF FIELD

Depth of field describes the area within which objects are in sharp critical focus. Although it is a technical term it also has aesthetic meaning.

The two factors affecting the depth of field are the lens focal length and lens aperture. Long lenses have a shallow depth of field and short lenses have a deep depth of field. For maximum depth the lens must be stopped down while a large aperture will narrow the focus.

The greater the depth of field, the more layers can be created from the front to the back of the frame. Shallow depth gives a flat surface effect while deep focus operates from front to back, as is seen in *Citizen Kane* (1941). The opposite effect is seen in *La Dolce Vita* (1960), which has no wide-angle shots.

CHANGING FOCUS

The focus of the frame may change when there is camera and/or subject movement. Following focus is when the operator must make adjustments in response to these changes. A focus pull or rack occurs when there is a deliberate change to which portion of the image is crisp and which is not. Using the diagram on page 152, the shallow focus example would change from person one in focus to person two and vice versa.

| – Exercise – |

Watch *Citizen Kane* (1941) and *La Dolce Vita* (1960) and consider how the deep and shallow focus affect your appreciation of the film. In what ways does the depth of field contribute to the story, characters or themes? Does the style suit the content? In other words, do the story and the way it is filmed work together to make a stronger film? If not, what would you do differently?

« 1: CITIZEN KANE
In this scene from *Citizen Kane* (1941) a short lens has been used to increase the deep depth of field from front to back.
Director: Orson Welles
RKO / The Kobal Collection

^ 2: DEPTH OF FIELD
In this scene from *Him Over There* a shallow depth of field has been created; the character in the foreground is in focus while the background is soft.
Student film-maker: John Vanderpuije

1: DEPTH OF FIELD AND APERTURE
With shallow depth of field (top) the character in the foreground is in focus, while the background is soft. With deep depth of field (bottom) both the foreground and background are in focus.

6 FAQs

Which format is better: film or digital?
It depends what you intend on filming. Film is the traditional and more expensive option for drama but there are some high-quality digital alternatives.

Why is lighting so important?
Light and shade create the impression of depth and nuance in the frame. Without lighting, the picture can look flat and dull.

Why do lights have coloured gels attached to them?
Sometimes the gels are a practical necessity to balance indoor and outdoor light sources. At other times they are used for creative effect to add visual interest and enhance the atmosphere.

Why change lenses for different shots or scenes?
It is possible to use just one lens to cover the whole film; however, using the best lens for the job means changing from short to long lens to cover the requirements of each scene effectively.

— Choosing what format to shoot on is a good starting point.

— Plan the framing and composition to be technically adept and visually interesting.

— Think about lighting design to add depth and atmosphere to the picture.

— Consider using coloured gels to either balance light sources or create dramatic effects.

— Experiment with focal length and aperture for deep and shallow focus.

Running glossary

Time code – an electronic signal recorded to identify each frame of tape. It is displayed as pairs of numbers separated by a colon (hours : minutes : seconds : frames)

Headroom – the space between the top of a subject's head and the top of the frame

Looking room – the space from the subject's eyeline toward the edge of the frame

Three point lighting – the key light, back light and fill light, which make up a basic lighting set-up

White balance – the function that adjusts the camera according to the light conditions

Depth of field – the range of sharp critical focus

≈ *1:* SOUND EFFECTS
Sound effects can be obtained from a range of sources. A lot of imagination is needed to come up with the best effects for the film.

7 SOUND

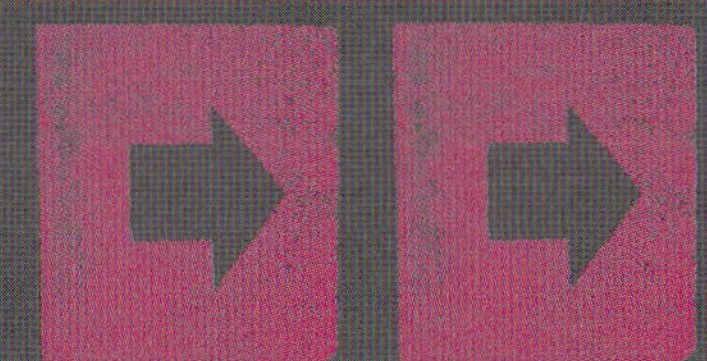

Sound is often considered the poor relation to picture in film-making. Starting as a silent medium without dialogue, films were typically screened accompanied by a pianist who played along, creating atmosphere and heightening the narrative elements. Today, sound includes the dialogue, background sound, voice-over, sound effects and music. All of these elements contribute to the story, characters and style of the film, and help to immerse the audience in the experience.

Diegesis means the narrative world of the film and film sound is often defined as either **diegetic** or **non-diegetic**. Diegetic sound is captured during the production process and originates from the objects or people within the world of the film. This includes sounds that exist in the interior world of the characters, such as thoughts. Non-diegetic sound comes from outside the world of the film, such as the musical soundtrack, and is captured during the post-production stage.

This chapter considers some of the practicalities of capturing sound and the many different ways that the audio works in a film.

Audio field production

Field audio is the sound that is recorded during production, such as the dialogue recorded by the production sound mixer during shooting. Later, the separate sound takes are edited together to produce a continuous soundtrack. **Synchronised sound** refers to the dialogue and sounds associated with the action, such as footsteps. Non-synchronised sound is the general background sound recording of a location known as **wild track**, which is helpful in the editing process to overlap and mix with other ingredients in the sound recipe.

The choice of location or studio shooting has clear implications for the sound department. Studios provide a controlled environment tailored to film-making, while real locations can be noisy and busy, which can interfere with the progress of the production.

When shooting on film the sound is recorded separately to the image (*see* Chapter 6), which is why it is essential to mark the shot with the clapperboard. The information written on the clapperboard identifies the shot visually and the verbal description does so audibly. The physical clap of the board enables the picture and sound to be synchronised during post-production. On digital formats the sound is recorded with the picture so they are already synchronised and identified by the time code. This means the tradition of the clapperboard is not technically necessary with digital.

The sound mixer and boom operator work as a team on the shoot, aiming to capture the best possible sound quality, the criteria of which includes a faithful and clear representation of the sound.

Sound recordings during production are crucial to the success of the film. In order to achieve good sound quality the levels are monitored during recording and if the sound recordist is dissatisfied more takes will be required until they are happy. Reasons for poor sound can be numerous; there may be interference caused by traffic noise, planes overhead, buzzing from power cables or noise from electrical sources such as lights and fridges.

1 – 2: LOCATION
When recording sounds, careful consideration must be taken with regards to the location of each scene and the sounds that the audience will expect to hear. Effective sound is integral to the meaning of the film.

– Exercise –

Listen to the room you are in: what can you hear? Even in an apparently silent room there will be some audible sound – the buzz of the lights, the hum of heating, the faint sound of traffic on the road outside. These all contribute to the sound profile of a space and every new space has a different one. That is why it is so important to capture the unique blend of sounds in each spot you film in.

Microphones

The human ear is highly selective and filters out extraneous sounds. So, if we are at a party full of conversations we tend to tune into the one that interests us the most and fade out the background sounds. The microphone does not have that ability, which means it is important to choose the best one for each job. The type of microphone used will depend on the function it is to perform.

The shape and mounting of the microphone affects the performance, so choosing the most appropriate microphone for the situation will greatly improve the recording. Different microphones record according to what is known as their 'pick up pattern', which refers to their directional characteristic. The three main pick up patterns are: omnidirectional (all directions), bidirectional (two directions) and unidirectional (one direction). Unidirectional pick up patterns include cardioid and hyper cardioid.

Omnidirectional microphones capture sound equally from all directions. They are good for general atmosphere but not for dialogue, unless the speaker is close by. This is because they pick up sound from behind as well as in front, so may record extraneous noise. Personal microphones are omnidirectional and include tie clips that are attached to the speaker. They produce high sound quality, but rustling clothing or accessories can create problems.

Bidirectional microphones use a figure of eight pattern and pick up sound equally from two opposite directions. These microphones tend to be used in situations such as interviews between two people facing each other, with the microphone placed between them.

Cardioid microphones are a type of unidirectional microphone that are used in interviews, performances and so on. These usually have a cardioid (heart-shaped) pick up pattern, which means they are more sensitive to the front and sides. They need to be held close to the sound source and consequently often appear in shot, making them unsuitable for some situations such as dramas. Certain sounds can be highlighted and others toned down with this type of microphone. Hand-held microphones have a cardioid pick up and are often used in interviews.

Gun microphones have a hyper cardioid pick up pattern. This type of pick up is very directional and eliminates most sound from the sides and rear. The longer the microphone the more directional its response tends to be. Gun microphones have an extendable boom pole attached, which means they must be aimed accurately at the source, requiring an adept operator who will adapt to any changes in position, movement, etc. Keeping the microphone as close to the sound source as possible without getting it in shot takes a great deal of skill. Gun microphones also pick up beyond the immediate source, so traffic and air conditioning can infringe as a result.

Sound recordists choose a combination of microphones depending on the practical, technical and aesthetic requirements. If a microphone position is changed within a scene it can alter the entire perspective and make the edit very tricky.

Wild track is recorded in every location filmed in so that the atmosphere or background sound can be captured. In addition, sound sources specific to each location, such as doors closing, traffic, etc. need to be recorded.

Good sound levels are essential; if levels are too low sound will be buried under tape hiss – too high and the louder sections will overload and distort. Levels should be checked during rehearsal, adjusted accordingly and consistently monitored.

When recording sound, it is important to bear in mind the possible problems that can be encountered. These include the fact that cable noise can sometimes pick up radio interference from taxi cabs, and electrical appliances such as lighting and fridges can cause background hum. All potential problems should be dealt with before shooting starts.

1: PICK UP PATTERNS
There are many different microphones available, these include (from top left to bottom right): omnidirectional, bidirectional, cardioid and hyper cardioid.

Post-production sound

Post-production is the stage when all of the sound sources are mixed together to create the final soundtrack. The levels of each sound are balanced so that key sounds can be promoted while others are used as background. The mix helps direct audience attention and can, for example, represent what one of the characters can hear. This is called point of audition and is an audio effect similar to the point of view shot for picture. The way the sounds are mixed is a highly skilled operation as the soundtrack must work with the pictures to create an effective film. Narration and voice-over are recorded during this stage, which can help connect scenes and provide rapid insight into the characters' inner thoughts.

Each sound source occupies a different track and a dubbing sheet is used to plan how and where each one appears, and how they overlap with each other. This is called track laying. The next stage is mixing, which is when the levels of each source are adjusted.

Overlapping sound can help make the transition from one setting to another more effective. If, for example, we hear a train pulling into the station before cutting to a corresponding image the edit seems smoother as the sound has paved the way for the image.

Non-verbal sound can be used to reinforce or contradict the visuals. In *Reservoir Dogs* (1992), for example, many sounds are amplified to be much louder than in reality. The sounds chosen for this treatment are ones with physical contact, such as a friendly slap on the back or a glass being placed on a desk. These are amplified while other more naturalistic sounds, such as the background atmosphere, are filtered out creating a highly stylised soundtrack that is consistent and therefore plausible in the context of the film.

Raging Bull (1980) is another example of creative sound mixing. During the fight scenes the sound is distorted to create the sense that the audience is inside the ring and even inside the head of the protagonist, Jake La Motta. This works in a similar way to a close-up shot in that it intensifies the scene and makes it intimate.

1 – 2: SOUND BOOTHS
Post-production sound is created in a controlled environment, such as in this sound-proof sound booth.

| – Exercise – |

Watch *Raging Bull* (1980) and make notes about the different sounds, where they appear and how they seem to be mixed to create different physical and emotional effects.

EVERLAST

⌃ 1: RESERVOIR DOGS
In this warehouse scene from *Reservoir Dogs* (1992), sounds are amplified for dramatic effect to increase the intensity of the situation.
Director: Quentin Tarantino
Live Entertainment/The Kobal Collection

« 2: RAGING BULL
In *Raging Bull* (1980) the sound in the ring is distorted during the fight scenes. This creates the sense of being in the protagonist's head.
Director: Martin Scorsese
United Artists/The Kobal Collection

The music used in a film can be powerful in recalling the film for the audience and is often exploited for marketing and promotional purposes. It can come from a variety of sources: a commercial band's recording repertoire, a copyright-free library audio, or it may even be specially composed.

The composer meets with the producer, director and music editor to decide where music will appear in the film. From there they build up music appropriate to the scene, for example, by thinking about which instruments create the type of sound that characterises the different stages and moods of the film. Music is an integral part of film to the extent that it often blends seamlessly with the picture without drawing attention to itself. It can be evocative and emotive, adding nuance and altering perception all at the same time. Using rhythm and tempo, melody or discordant tones, the music conveys mood and emotion enhancing character and story. Max Steiner wrote the first original score in 1933 for *King Kong*, in which he worked to illustrate the story through a range of techniques that are still in operation today.

One of these techniques is leitmotif, which is the term used to describe a recurrent theme throughout a composition that is associated with a particular person, idea or situation. One of the most famous examples of leitmotif today is the two-note theme that is heard every time the shark approaches in *Jaws* (1975).

Film music composition is a specialist area attracting talented musicians to create unique soundtracks. Well known composers working today include Ry Cooder, Ennio Morricone, Danny Elfman and Michael Nyman.

Popular songs take advantage of the prior associations attached to them and can emphasise the characters' thoughts and feelings. However, if using an existing music track the rights must be cleared before it can be included. Depending on the source this can be a very time-consuming and costly operation.

Library music consists of tracks specially compiled for use in film. It is much more straightforward to obtain, which means less time and money are spent. Library music can be very useful for documentary and film-makers who are working on a limited budget.

The type of music and the way it is used is often dependent on film genre. The soundtrack for a spaghetti western is very different to that of a thriller, but both use aural motifs that create mood, suspense and indicate time and genre. Whatever the genre, films tend to follow certain conventions that make them instantly recognisable to the audience, such as love songs in romance films.

Reservoir Dogs (1992) subverted this convention by clashing the screen action with the emotion of the music. During scenes of violence and tension an upbeat pop tune plays, making the scene even more difficult to watch because the violence is exaggerated by being in contrast to the music.

Another inventive way in which music has been used for effect is in *There's Something About Mary* (1998), where the film parodies the way in which music appears in many films without a motivated source. Whenever the background music plays, a shot of a band of minstrels performing the piece appears in the scene.

– Exercise –

Listen to the sound in *Star Wars* (1977) and *The Lord of The Rings* (2001) and identify the different leitmotifs. What is the tone of each and how do they contribute to character development and story?

Think about the different ways music can be used in film, for example as theme tunes, background or part of the action. Watch *Reservoir Dogs* (1992) and make notes on the way music is used.

Sound effects

A sound effect is a non-verbal sound that can be created in a studio or obtained from a sound library. A range of effects can be mixed on the soundtrack to soothe and gladden or depress and menace. For example, the background sound of drilling will produce a different effect that of birdsong. These can be useful shortcuts as the audience will automatically make connections between the sound and the context. In crime or thriller genres the sound of rain lashing down immediately helps set the scene.

Spot effects, such as doors opening and closing, footsteps or the sound of a knock at the door, are usually recorded on-location. In addition to these, many sound effects are recorded during post-production on a **Foley stage**.

There is a lot of imagination involved in creating sound effects. For example, melons being sliced, smashed and squelched come in very handy for fight sequences. For the sinking of the ship in *Titanic* (1997), the sound effects team recorded a sheet of ice breaking mixed with other smashing sounds. The boulder in *Raiders of the Lost Ark* (1981) was created by rolling a car down a driveway, and the sound of alien spaceships in *Independence Day* (1996) was produced by screaming baboons. A fantastic array of sounds can be built up and mixed to create weird and wonderful effects.

| – Exercise – |

Think about what sound effects could be used to replicate the sound of fireworks. Try making the effects from everyday objects that you have to hand.

7 FAQs

Why can't I use the on-board camera microphone?
There is a microphone attached to most digital format cameras, which is suitable for domestic use; however, the sound quality will not be high enough for anything more.

How can I make sure the microphone doesn't get into the shot?
It is important to monitor the frame to ensure it does not creep in accidentally at any time.

Will I be able to adjust poor sound during the post-production?
Some degree of manipulation is possible during editing, but there are limits. For example, background sounds may be mixed down, but low levels on dialogue will need to be recorded again. It is important to get the best quality sound recording in the first instance.

Can I use a well-known pop song on my soundtrack?
Using existing music is possible, but the music rights have to be cleared, which means gaining the permission of the recording artists' publisher and paying a fee for the use of the track in question.

Checklist

—
Choose the most suitable microphone for the situation.

—
Carry out sound tests to check the equipment is recording properly and levels are set accurately.

—
Record a wild track in each of the locations you film in.

—
Consider having music composed specifically for your film, if possible, as it will provide a unique enhancement. It will also spare you the minefield of music copyright, which is necessary to get existing tracks cleared.

—
Make creative use of everyday objects as sound effects.

Running glossary

Diegetic – elements that are produced from within the fictional world in which the story takes place

Non-diegetic – elements that are created outside the world of the film, such as voice-overs and soundtracks

Synchronised sound – sound recorded at the same time as shooting the picture

Wild track – background sound recorded in each location

Foley stage – where post-production sound effects are recorded. Named after Jack Foley who mastered the technique of recording sound effects in synchronisation with the picture

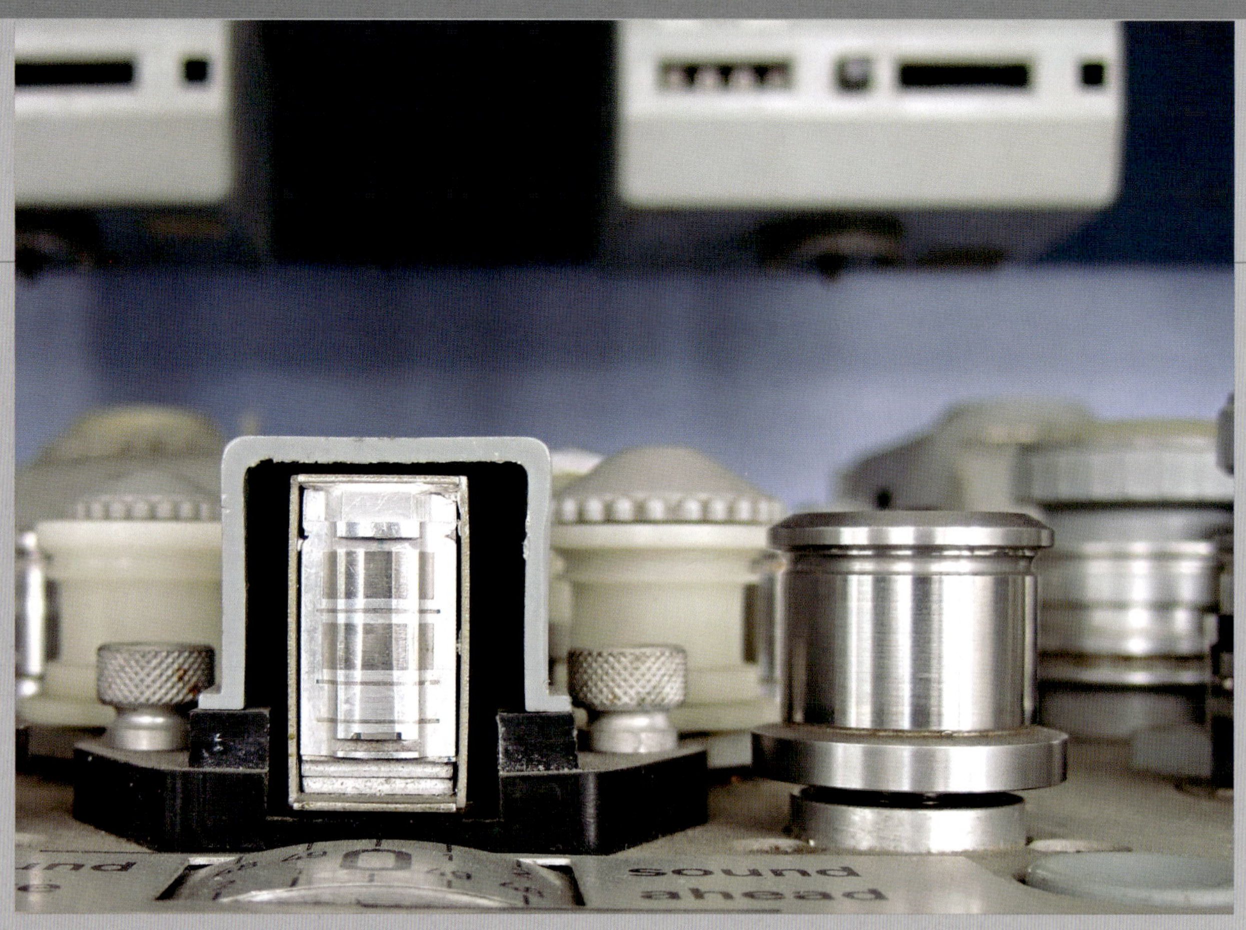

1: EDIT CONTROLS
During the editing process, all of the hard work from the production stages is brought together.

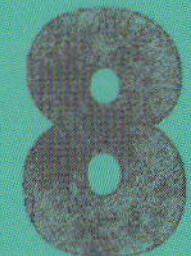

8 POST-PRODUCTION

When production is finished and the film is shot the post-production phase begins. This is when the editor puts all of the footage that has been filmed out of sequence back into the correct order so that is makes narrative sense. During this period the sound effects, music and titles are also included.

The editor brings together the skill and craft of the production team in the edit suite creating a coherent whole from their collective efforts. Whether a documentary, short or feature-length film, the editor works closely with the director to find a rhythm that complements the style and content of the footage.

This chapter looks at the techniques employed during post-production and traces the roots of two key approaches to editing: continuity and montage.

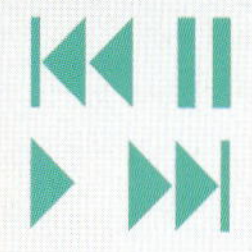

Editing is the joining of two shots together in a certain combination to establish the structure and rhythm of the film. The shots the editor chooses and the order in which they are combined sets the space and time of the film and guides the audience's attention. The way in which images are joined can produce shock, excitement and fascination. For example, suspense can be created through the use of short shots edited at a fast pace. Expectation can be set-up by cutting from one shot to another and back again several times before suddenly replacing one of the established shots with a new one.

For the first thirty years film was a silent medium, which meant that editing was concerned with the visual alone. D.W. Griffith pioneered **continuity editing** in America while Soviet film-makers Eisenstein, Pudovkin and Kuleshov experimented with **montage** techniques. These early film-makers recognised the potential of editing to change the emotional and intellectual responses to a film.

Editing technology is such that the digital manipulation of images has become the norm. By using digital systems such as AVID or Final Cut Pro each shot can be viewed on-screen, trimmed and repositioned with relative ease.

Film editing begins with making a work print (called rushes or dailies) from the processed negative. The work print is first edited then the negative is cut to match the work print. This is called negative matching or conforming. In the past the film was cut and spliced together by hand on an editing desk where the spools of film were laced up. Today film is often edited digitally, which means it is converted to a digital form during editing and converted back to film afterwards.

Whether using film or digital format the principles of editing remain the same. The editor lists all of the footage, which is called logging. The edit log catalogues the material using time code (*see* page 131) to identify the beginning and end of each take. When this is done shots are selected and combined to form a rough cut, known as the 'off line'. The fine cut or 'on line' edit is created when the editor is satisfied all of the sequences work together to create the overall finished film version.

Sound continues the illusion of continuity. The dialogue, background noise, sound effects and music all support the ideas in the script and enhance the end product. Music and sound influence the visuals and how we read them because they can provide information that is not overt in the picture. Sound is used to make the image credible within the world of the film, for example, the noise of people and traffic on a New York street can seem very real, even if the scene has been shot a million miles from New York City.

1: **BATTLESHIP POTEMKIN**
The Odessa Steps is a landmark scene in *Battleship Potemkin* (1925), which is itself an excellent example of the juxtaposition of images through montage editing.
Director: Sergei M Eisenstein
Goskin/The Kobal Collection

The majority of editing adheres to the conventions of continuity editing, which is where the shots are ordered according to narrative time. This maintains the appearance of a continuous flow in space and time. A typical sequence includes establishing shots, closer shots which direct the attention of the audience to key points in the narrative, followed by long shots which re-establish the place/setting. The change in camera position from a master shot to a closer shot, then a cutaway or a reaction, is read as continuous action by the audience.

In most mainstream films the edits are invisible and the images appear to flow in a continuous fashion. The continuity from shot to shot must be maintained to give the impression of a continuous time period so action, vision and sound all have to tie in for the illusion to work. When these rules are broken the result is a **jump cut**, which is a noticeable **transition** because the screen continuity is ruptured.

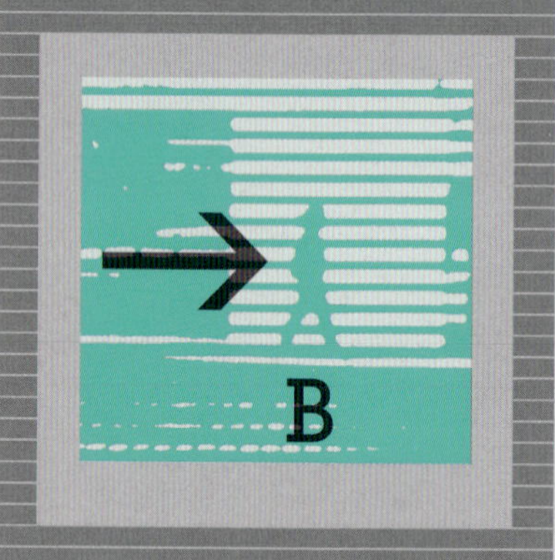

⌃ 1: 180 DEGREE RULE
If the camera is placed to the left of the person (A), they appear to be facing left in the direction of the arrow. If the camera is moved to the right of the person (B), they appear to be facing in the opposite direction. This is known as crossing the line (*see* page 78).

The 180 degree rule (*see* page 77) must also be adhered to in editing if the illusion of screen space and time is to be maintained. Crossing the line confuses the audience and contradicts what they have just seen. For example, if a person is walking across the screen from right to left the line is established in that direction. If the next shot is taken from the other side of the line the person will suddenly appear to be walking in the opposite direction, from left to right (*see* diagram opposite). Unless the editor wants to create this effect deliberately they must consistently use shots from one side of the line.

Overlapping the speech and image can help create a more fluid impression on-screen. For example, in a conversation between two people it looks more natural when the reaction shot comes before the end of the speaker's sentence. This is because it can look too mechanical making the edit point at the beginning and end of the dialogue. In a conversation, editors will try and cut shots that match, which means they are from a similar lens angle, distance and depth of field to each other. Conversely, on a single character sequence the editor will try and avoid cutting directly to a shot with the same camera angle because it can create a jump. In this case a different angle or a cutaway of something else in between works better. The headroom (*see* page 133) in the shot should remain consistent otherwise it can look like the character's height has changed.

| – *Exercise* – |

Watch the opening sequence of *Psycho* (1960) and break it down shot by shot. Deconstructing the shots in this way can help you see exactly how they have been put together and the effects that certain choices have made.

Manipulating time

The first films produced were made up of a single shot, where the camera stayed in one position and recorded what happened in front of it in real time. The screen time was the same then as the real time it took to record the scene, which limited what was possible to show in approximately two hours of screen time. As film-making developed and became more sophisticated film time was manipulated to speed up or slow down events. This allowed a more creative use of time, where information could be conveyed in a few shots that may have taken hours in real time.

Another technique used to manipulate time is parallel action, which is a convention that cuts between two situations in different places suggesting that they are happening simultaneously. In *Titanic* (1997), for example (*see* pages 84–85), the sinking ship is intercut with Rose immersed in the rising water; each time the water is seen to be getting higher the sense of urgency for Rose to escape is increased.

TRANSITIONS

A transition is the way that two images are joined together. There are a number of ways that this can be achieved and each of these options creates a different effect and subsequent meaning.

A cut is a clean change from one shot to another. This is the most commonly used transition and the most unobtrusive.

A mix or dissolve is a gradual transition from one shot to the next with the speed of the overlapping of images varying. This can be used to indicate a change in time or location or suggest links between the two images conceptually. A visual similarity can be very effective, for example, an eye morphing into the moon or a ceiling fan that morphs into the blades of a helicopter and so on.

A fade in or out is a gradual transition from the image to black (or another colour) or vice versa. This transition is often used at the beginning or end of a scene or film to signify the start or finish of an idea, chapter or story.

A wipe is where one part of the screen moves across the other, which can take the form of various patterns like swirls, stars, zig zags and so on. The classic wipe across the screen is a stylised way to show a change of place, for example, when the action jumps from one city to another.

CONCEPT

The edit can be used to suggest an idea that has not been made explicit. For example, a shot of a woman in child labour cut with a doctor talking to a distraught husband creates the idea that there is a problem and either the child, the woman or both are unhealthy or even dead.

MOTIVATION

As discussed previously (*see* Chapter 6) choices are motivated, which means there is a reason to choose a transition at a particular point in the flow of shots. Action, sound or both are good reasons to edit. Each shot contains visual information and each edit should provide further information that helps build-up the story. Decisions about when to cut and how long to leave each shot can be influenced by the type of film it is. For example, an action sequence will include lots of fast cuts to help create tension, suspense and excitement.

DEALING WITH SHORTCOMINGS

Editors have to work with what they are given which means they are sometimes disappointed by the absence of key shots. In addition to missing shots they also have to work around poorly shot material where the composition is weak, the camera shakes or the shot is just not held for long enough. The skilled editor finds solutions to these problems.

| – *Exercise* – |

Storyboard the scene below using no more than 12 shots to tell the story.

A person cycling from London to Brighton.

SOUND

Sound edits can be cut ahead or behind the picture to convey feelings such as tension or emotion. The sound edit can be very effective when it is made a few frames before the picture as this helps create interest and audience anticipation.

TITLES

The title sequence at the beginning of a film helps set-up audience expectation about what sort of film it will be. Usually the titles appear with the music, which further adds to the mood and emotion. The choice of font, lighting, colours and the pace that they are edited together all contribute to the mood. *Bond* films always begin with a big show-stopping title sequence and theme tune.

The titles at the end of most films tend to be less imaginative; however, there are plenty of examples where the closing credits continue the tone of the whole film right to the last frame. Comedies often include out-takes with the end credits.

1: TITLE SEQUENCE
The title sequence of a film can help to establish the mood and style of what is to follow. The instantly recognisable gun barrel shot from the *Bond* films always forms part of the opening title sequence.
Danjaq/EON/UA/The Kobal Collection

CONTINUITY EDITING TECHNIQUES

The 180 degree rule
The imaginary line that passes from side to side through the actors.

Parallel editing
Cross-cutting between two or more lines of action going on in different places.

Matching eyelines
An edit following the 180 degree rule, in which the first shot shows a person looking in one direction and the second shows the space containing what the person sees.

Match on action
An edit that puts two different shots of the same action together making it appear to continue uninterrupted.

Shot, reverse, shot
Two shots edited back and forth between two characters.

30 degree rule
The angle between two camera positions should not be less than 30 degrees in order to avoid a jump cut.

Exercise

Watch any of the films listed for post-production in the Appendix (*see* page 200). Decide how the narrative space and characters have been established. In other words, look at the direction, position, distance continuity or relationship that is communicated with each transition.

Change the order and put these shots in the order you think is the most effective.

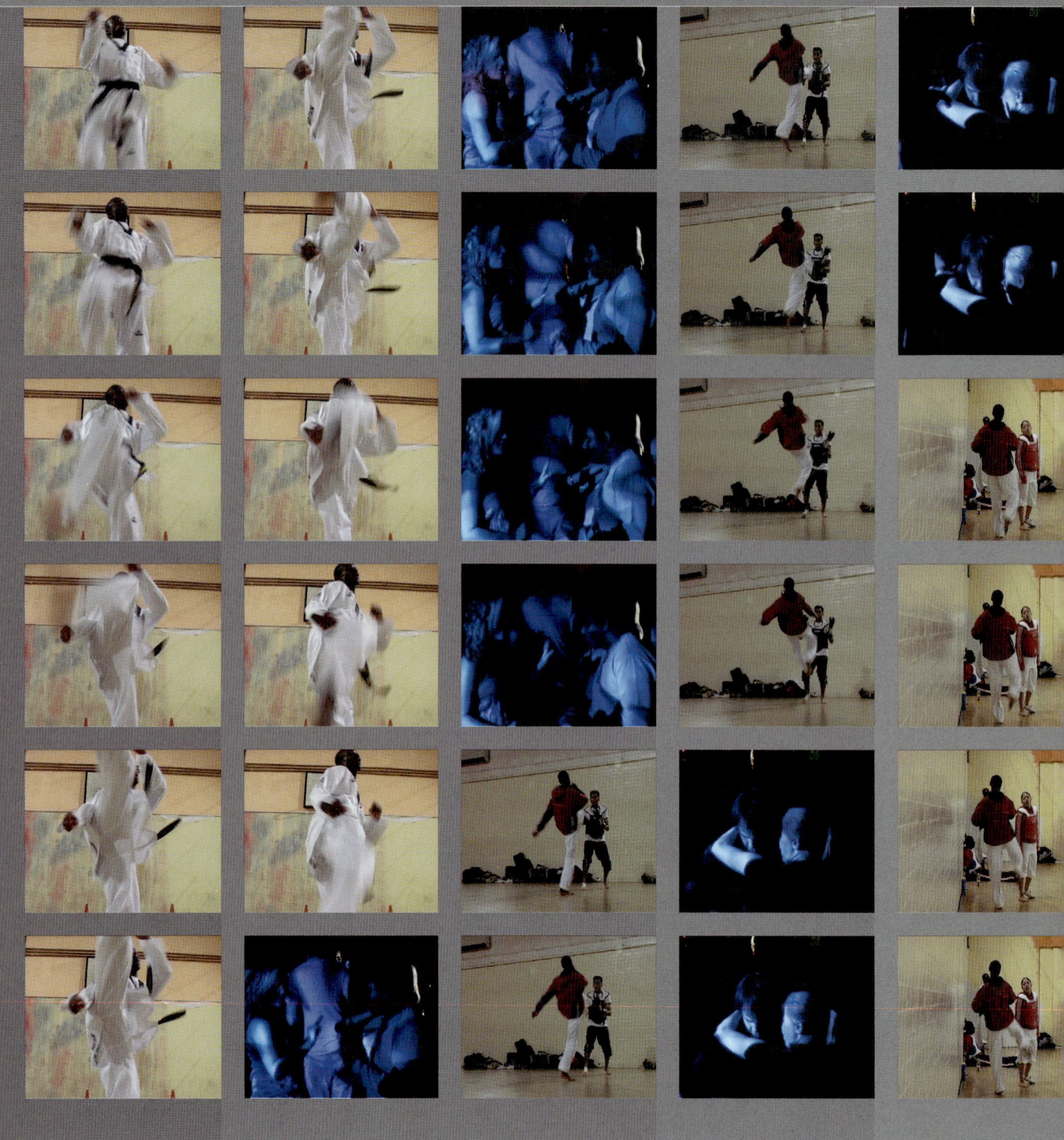

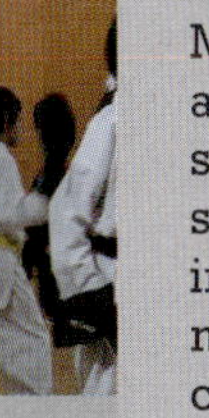

Montage is the joining of two shots to produce a third meaning greater than the individual shots. This is a more expressive form than simply putting shots in a sequence because it intentionally adds depth. The aim is not to mimic reality, but to draw attention to ideas by clashing shots to create a deeper meaning.

« 1: MONTAGE EDITING
These shots from *Romaine Focused* are a good example of montage editing. The nightclub scenes are juxtaposed with the tae kwon do training (top to botom, column by column) to create a new meaning.
Student Film-Maker: Johannes Hausen

Soviet film-makers Eisenstein, Pudovkin and Kuleshov first experimented with montage techniques in the 1920s. The Kuleshov experiment involved Kuleshov filming an actor, a bowl of soup, a girl playing with a teddy bear and a woman in a coffin. He edited the shots in different sequences and asked an audience to respond. The shot of the actor was the same in each sequence, but the audience interpreted his mood differently depending on which shots he was juxtaposed with. Hence the audience read the same shot as conveying thoughtfulness (soup), joy (child) and sorrow (coffin) when it was the same shot used every time. This forms the basis of montage theory; the order in which shots are combined influences our perception. The brain makes connections between objects when viewed together and each shot derives meaning from the context it is placed in.

Sergei Eisenstein tried to challenge the audience further by combining shots that did not have an apparent connection to create what he called 'associations'. Often an act is suggested through montage that is not made explicit in the action, but the association makes it seem complete. To use a gory example, we often see people being shot or stabbed on film without actually seeing the point of contact. One shot presents the image of the person firing the gun, while in the next cut we see the person it was aimed at falling to the floor. These images combine to imply the person has been shot.

Montage disrupts the narrative flow by colliding disparate images; it is unlike continuity editing, which aims to convey a continuous flow of space and time. In montage the juxtaposition of images can often be disturbing or challenging. The Odessa Steps is a landmark scene in Eisenstein's *Battleship Potemkin* (1925) in which a baby in a pram goes flying out of control down the steps during a riot. This scene is an example of rapid cutting. For Eisenstein the illusion of talking people went against the principles of his work. He argued that sound, rather than attempting to imitate reality, should bring out meaning not evident in the images alone.

Today the term montage is usually used to mean sequences where shots are edited to condense a period of time, for example, a blossoming relationship that takes weeks or months is portrayed in a few minutes of short successive shots.

There are forms of editing that do not adhere to the rules of continuity editing and have continued the Soviet tradition of exploration. Generally these tend to be used more in film that does not rely on narrative to make sense. Artist film, experimental work and music videos, for example, often use different techniques that deliberately draw attention to the edits, thus making the construction visible. Documentary often indicates that an interview has been edited by using jump cuts to show breaks in the flow such as in Scorsese's documentary *No Direction Home: Bob Dylan* (2005).

| – *Exercise* – |

A man walks into a butcher's shop and asks for a sheep's head. He leaves the shop and cycles home. Draw a storyboard for this scene trying to break as many of the rules of continuity editing as possible.

Continuous shot

1: CONTINUITY EDITING
This example of continuity editing has no sharp cuts, which gives the impression of continuous time (top to botom, column by column). This is in direct contrast with the sharp edits in the montage sequence on pages 178–179.

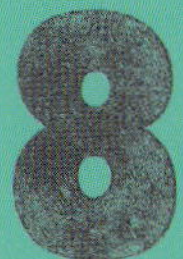

FAQs

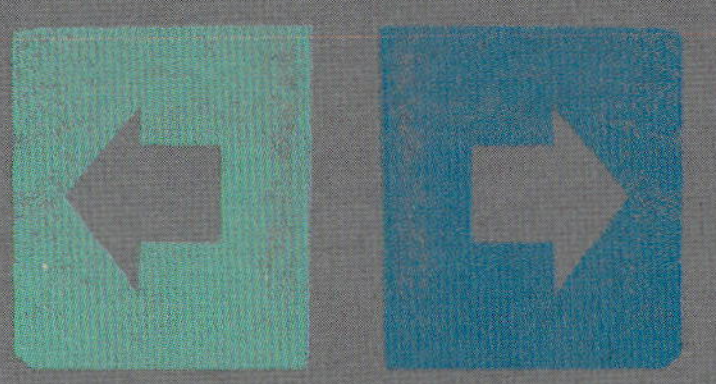

What is a transition?
It is the method of joining the shots.

How does editing manipulate the images we see?
By changing the order of images, editing can place events out of chronological order. By following continuity editing, spatial relationships are influenced and appear different to reality. Often this manipulation of time and space is for dramatic purpose to help tell a story more effectively.

How can I work around poor footage?
If possible arrange to have a reshoot, where essential shots that were missed the first time can be picked up. If this is not possible you will need to work with what you have trimming where necessary. Make a list of the types of shots that you need this time and refer to it in the future.

Why should I follow the rules of continuity editing?
It is useful to learn and master them as they are required for the large majority of editing work. Once you have mastered them you can play with breaking the rules.

Checklist

— Editing is the selection and combination of picture and sound in a certain order at a certain pace.

— The editor logs the rushes before starting to edit, that way they know exactly what footage they have to work with.

— The rough cut allows them to experiment with different ideas before committing to the fine cut/final edit.

— Whatever system or format is used the principles of editing remain the same.

— Looking at other films and breaking down the shots is a good way for an editor to learn their craft.

— Once the rules of continuity editing have been learnt they can be experimented with for creative effect.

Running glossary

Continuity editing – joining together separate shots during post-production to create the illusion of continuous time and space

Montage – the selection and combination of shots into a sequence. Pioneered by the Soviet film-makers of the 1920s who were experimenting with how the joining of two shots could create a third meaning greater than the individual shots

Jump cut – an edit that disrupts the illusion of continuous screen time

Transition – the change between one shot and another (e.g. cut, dissolve, fade and wipe)

1: FILM THEORY
The study of film theory includes a number of approaches, from the history of technological innovations in sound and colour to the study of film form for particular directors.
Copyright: Tatiana Morozova

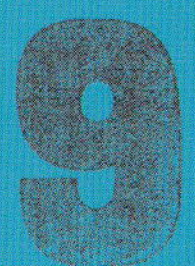

Chapter 9

MAKING MEANING

Film production students have been known to complain about how boring and unnecessary film theory can be. They do not understand how theorists have read into the content in such a detailed and seemingly bizarre fashion. It is true that theorists analyse text and find meaning that may not have been intended by the maker. However, the film image is not accidental and there are codes and conventions used in its creation. Film is a process involving many people; the choices made impact on the film and its meaning in both intentional and unintentional ways.

Film communicates to the audience through film language and film technique relies on technical and creative choices of film stock, camera angle, depth of field, format, framing, lighting position, intensity and motivation. The film-maker is rarely just recording what is in front of them but enhancing and dramatising to produce a more effective story and mood.

What follows are some fundamental starting points to looking at film theory with a very brief introduction to the ways in which meaning is invested in film.

Documentary

The term documentary refers to a programme that provides a factual report on a given subject – it is an attempt to document reality. Documentary has its history in the first films of the Lumière brothers and John Grierson and can be found in movements such as Free Cinema and Cinéma Vérité.

Whose story is being told by whom has enormous influence over the way in which ideas, events and characters are represented. It is helpful for the audience to know what perspective a story is coming from as it helps inform our understanding and interpretation. Documentary point of view tends to fall into one of the following categories: objective (not influenced by personal opinions or feelings), subjective (influenced by personal opinions or feelings), polemic (an attack on someone or something) or propaganda (biased or misleading to promote a political cause or point of view).

Four main approaches have been identified in documentary. The 'expository' uses traditional documentary techniques, such as voice-over to narrate the story. In this approach, the audience is told what is going on through a convention known as the 'Voice of God' because it is authoritative and, we are led to believe, accurate and truthful. Early documentaries such as those of John Grierson exemplify this approach.

The 'observational' or 'fly on the wall' approach is where the camera records events as they unfold without any intervention. The film-makers do not appear in-frame or impose their interpretation of events through voice-over. This creates the illusion that the camera is invisible, which can be problematic because it doesn't acknowledge how people respond when a camera is present or how the camera alters the situation being recorded. Often scenes are set-up for the camera and are presented as natural. This raises questions around how much the film-maker should intervene and invites debate about authenticity and ethics.

The 'interactive' approach uses interviews to help build a sense of character and story. This can create a biased impression because of the way the interviewer can manipulate the subject. The film-maker and director Nick Broomfield uses this approach and is always present in his documentaries, privileging his perspective over the interviewees' own.

The 'reflexive' approach plays with the codes and conventions of documentary making by drawing attention to the seams of its own construction. This leads the audience to question and be more active in interpreting the ethics, impartiality and intentions of the film-maker. Examples of this approach include Dziga Vertov's *Man With A Movie Camera* (1929), and films by Brecht and Jean-Luc Godard.

⌃ 1: DOCUMENTARY
In *Paul Merton in China* (2007), the audience is shown a subjective portrayal of the country through the eyes of Paul Merton.
Director: Barbie MacLaurin
Tiger Aspect Productions

| – Exercise – |

Consider the brief below and how it would appear differently on the screen when made in each of the four documentary modes.

An asylum seeker is about to be deported and sent back to their country of origin where they will face the death sentence.

Representation

Cinema constructs meaning through representing characters and stories, making representation a key area of film study. Every image we see is a representation constructed from choices made during the course of the production process. These choices include the genre characteristics that the film has; the narrative structure; and how film language (camera, sound, design etc) is employed. All of the decisions made throughout the stages of production alter the meaning of the film. Crucially, however, readings differ depending on the audience and their particular experiences and expectations.

To analyse the way a film constructs representations we can consider whether the characters have depth and values. Areas of particular concern in relation to characters are gender, race and class representation. This is because these issues are considered sites of struggle over meaning.

The audience makes sense of characters based on visual aspects like their appearance the setting and costume – all of which have been constructed during the production of the film. As a result, films help to build perceptions about what we consider 'normal' and can influence expectations about different people and their behaviour.

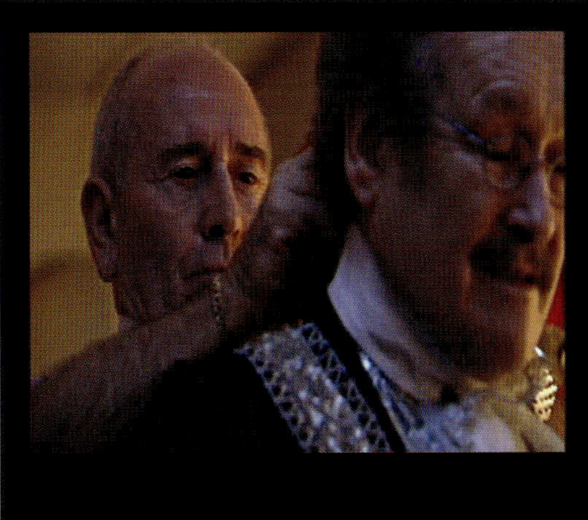

1 – 2: REPRESENTATION
3-Minute Wonders: It's Behind You is a tragicomic series of documentaries that explores fame and celebrity and what happens when they start to fade.
Tiger Aspect Productions

– Exercise –

Make two columns and list everything you know about George Bush in one and Osama Bin Laden in the other. What are your impressions based on? How accurate do you think they are likely to be? Depending on what country you live in the list will alter according to the way each of these figures has been represented in the media. This indicates the meanings are not fixed, but open to interpretation depending on cultural context.

Realist film critics such as André Bazin, Siegfried Kracauer and Stanley Cavell consider film to be a photographic representation of reality able to accurately capture the world we live in. They favour techniques of authenticity such as the long take and deep focus photography.

Formalists such as Sergei Eisenstein and Rudolf Arnheim, on the other hand, argue that film cannot capture reality accurately and that is what makes it worthy as a form of art; its limitations enable it to convey artistic vision. Formalist film-makers highlight the lack of realism through the use of montage (*see* Chapter 8) to deliberately expose the film-making process.

The realists try to retain real time and space, while the formalists deliberately manipulate it to remind the audience that what they are watching is not real, but a constructed representation.

Film records events that take place in front of the camera. These events often appear realistic in that they take place in a real place where actors pretend to be real people. Realism is a cinematic convention that we have come to accept in the same way we accept the perspective provided in a painting. Fictional representations inform our view of the world and should not necessarily be accepted as real.

Hollywood realism uses techniques such as continuity editing (*see* Chapter 8) and the construction of a believable setting to confer its credentials. Continuity editing creates a coherent sense of space and time on-screen through use of techniques such as point of view, matching eyelines and directional continuity. The editing contributes to the sense of the film-maker's invisibility, creating the illusion of continuous time and space, all of which helps to support the suspension of disbelief that is central to the enjoyment of the film.

A major part of film-making involves the interaction between mise en scène (the arrangement and composition of design, lighting and actors in front of the camera) and mise en shot (the way the events are filmed).

» 1: REALISM
In *Man on the Moon* (2006) the setting and costume contribute to create a sense of realism.
Director: Rupert Edwards

Exercise

Look at the film set on page 115. What is your first impression of the place/setting? Write down the props and dressings that have been used. Why do you think they have been chosen and positioned in the frame in the way they have been? What sort of people do you expect to see here? What sort of story might take place in this space? How realistic do you think the picture is? Can you see the way meaning has been created through the codes of construction?

Genre is a French word meaning 'type'. Most films can be categorised according to their genre, which has proved a useful approach for film analysis. Films adhere to a set of narrative and representational conventions within each genre, which audiences recognise and understand. These genres include western, musical, crime, horror, comedy, romance and science fiction, each of which has its own set of anticipated plots, situations, characters, costumes, dialogue, setting, props and style. The reoccurring patterns are familiar and comforting in their predictability. Film marketing and publicity rely on genre to help promote films by identifying with the previous success of that genre to sell the film.

However, genre conventions are not fixed – they adapt according to changes in society. For example, a contemporary western has similarities with the classic western, but it has also changed over time.

Genre can be seen to replay the cultural myths and fantasies of adventure and romance. Mainstream classic narrative – where the major protagonist works through problems and obstacles that create tension and conflict to find solutions – is reproduced in the majority of genres. The hero goes on some kind of a journey, defeats the villain, rescues the woman and is victorious. These solutions often support the dominant value system in society, such as the importance and status attached to the accumulation of wealth.

Genre study examines the patterns of repetition in film and challenges the auteur theory's privileging of the director as artist, dwelling instead on the industrial character of film production. In practice, both auteur theory and genre theory can be seen to contribute to the understanding of a film. For example, Hitchcock produced films within the thriller genre whilst also weaving many themes unique to his particular world view into his work. This can be seen in *The Wrong Man* (1956), where the thriller is interwoven with themes of Catholic guilt and misogyny.

» 1: GENRE
The genre of a film is instantly recognisable to the audience due to the reoccurring patterns of plot, situations, characters, dialogue, costume, setting, props and style.
Copyright: Daniel Padavona

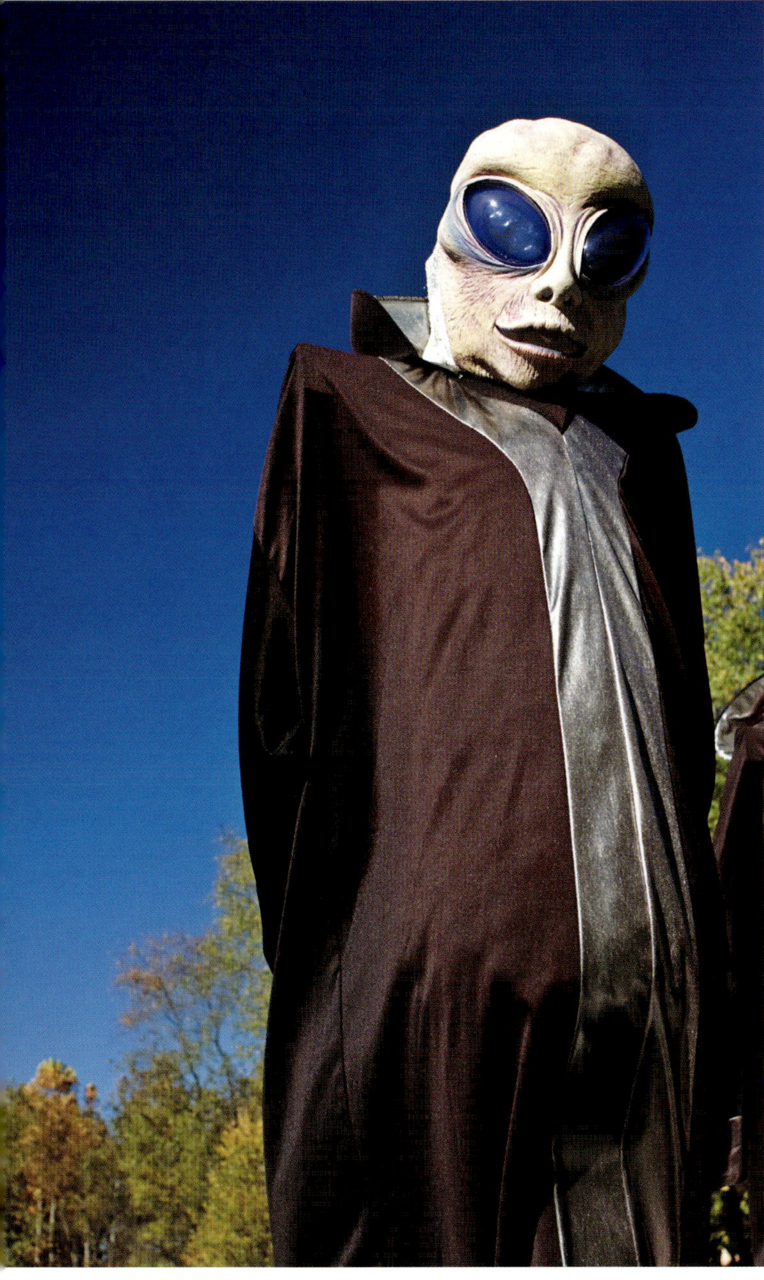

| – Exercise – |

Consider these directors, list the genres they tend to work in and the recurring themes that have become their trademark.

Pedro Almodóvar, Jane Campion, Martin Scorsese and Tim Burton.

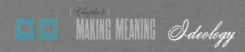

Ideology is a term used to describe a set of beliefs, such as capitalism or socialism, that influence behaviour. It refers to the values and meanings that are communicated in the cultural products of society, such as film. It does not always emerge directly mirroring just one set of clearly defined values, but often represents a range of competing notions that are constantly evolving and renegotiating their boundaries.

Each time a story is told it is through the cultural context of time, which is constantly changing. Film tells stories and communicates beliefs through the stories and the way they are told. The values of the storytellers filter into the film in conscious and unconscious ways, the function of which is the source of research by people such as Claude Levi-Strauss, Vladimir Propp, Roland Barthes and Stuart Hall. Levi-Strauss found in his study of myth that it was comprised of binary oppositions such as good and evil, black and white, and hero and villain. These opposites create a tension that produces conflict, the working out of which results in the narrative at the heart of myth.

One of the conventions of genre is an identifiable ideology. For example, in a thriller normality is disrupted by a crime that is represented in such a way that the audience disapproves of it. Consequently, our sympathies rest with the characters trying to solve the crime. Narrative closure usually comes with the solving of the crime, and the capture and punishment of the criminal.

Ideological values are inherent in the text, but often these are not obvious or overt to us. As viewers we read these conventions as being natural and normal, because they are effectively embedded in the text. For example, a mainstream, commercially produced film will have key characters who hold particular views. The extent to which these are raised and questioned in the text indicates the film-maker's position and intended meaning. Who are the protagonists and antagonists and what do they want? As discussed in Chapter 2: Scriptwriting, the protagonist is usually the hero, the antagonist the villain. The hero is usually at the heart of the film, driving the narrative forward.

We, the audience, identify with the characters in the film and experience the ups and downs of their journey. The characters we identify with are usually those who share our values and ideologies. Each audience member brings a unique combination of experiences to a film, which means the subsequent reading of the film will depend on those variables.

« 1: IDEOLOGY IN DOCUMENTARY
The ideological values of a film are embedded in the imagery employed by the film-maker, as in *Man on the Moon* (2006).
Director: Rupert Edwards

Auteur theory

Auteur theory views the director as central to the making of meaning. During the 1950s, the French journal *Cahiers du Cinéma* criticised the cinema of the period as formulaic. François Truffaut in particular wrote that French cinema merely reproduced scripts on to the screen without any personality or visual flare. In contrast the auteur created a unique interpretation and manipulated the mise en scène in order to put their mark on the script and give it an identity tied to their own set of values. Alfred Hitchcock is considered one of the ultimate auteurs because of the consistent themes and style across the body of his work.

Directors who have consistent styles and themes are called auteurs. As we have seen, a film crew involves many people who contribute and influence the end product; however, auteur theory claims it is the director who makes the crucial choices that determine the way the film appears on the screen.

Many of the critics from *Cahiers du Cinéma* went on to make films in the 1960s, which embodied improvisation and spontaneity. They were known as 'The French New Wave' and included the directors Truffaut, Godard, Chabrol, Rohmer, Rivette. The French New Wave is considered to be one of the major European Cinema movements exemplified by the film *À bout de souffle* (1960) by Jean-Luc Godard.

1: À BOUT DE SOUFFLE
À bout de souffle (1960) is a seminal example of the work of Jean-Luc Godard, who is one of the most famous of the auteurs in film-making.
Director: Jean-Luc Godard
Getty Images

– Exercise –

Many film scripts are available online and in libraries. Obtain a script for a film you are familiar with and consider the differences between the film you know and the original script. You may be surprised at the details that have been changed. On the other hand the script may appear as an exact blueprint for the film. Consider how much influence the director has had on the film and whether you think they deserve to be called an auteur.

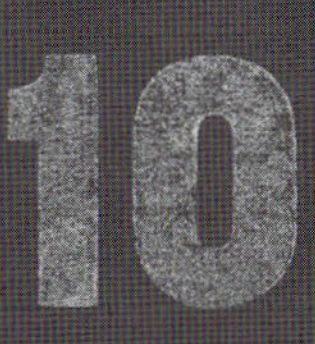

10 APPENDIX

Essential viewing

THE TEAM

There are several films to watch that help illustrate how the roles come together in practice. The following examples take the audience behind the scenes revealing the intricate workings of a film production crew.

Living In Oblivion (1995)
Essential viewing for all budding film-makers, this is a comedy about the making of a film, which takes place during one day of a low-budget shoot.

A Cock and Bull Story (2005)
Director Michael Winterbottom attempts to make the adaptation of Laurence Sterne's essentially unfilmable novel, *The Life and Opinions of Tristram Shandy, Gentleman*.

The Player (1992)
A studio executive is blackmailed by a writer whose script he rejected; but which one? Bursting with behind the scenes Hollywood insider jokes.

Get Shorty (1995)
When John Travolta's mobster character goes to Hollywood to collect a debt, he discovers that the movie business is much the same as his current source of employment.

Day for Night (1973)
A film company at work and all the complications that arise on the set and off – things can get messy!

DIRECTION

Below is a selection of films that show striking examples of direction, covering a diverse range of styles. Skillful direction is capable of creating compelling cinematic worlds.

The Godfather (1972)
Francis Ford Coppola's stunning first in the trilogy uses powerful direction that doesn't pull any punches.

Wings of Desire (1987)
This beautiful and evocative Wim Wenders' film creates a world where angels listen to the thoughts of mortals, monitor their souls and fall in love with them.

The Hustler (1961)
Robert Rossen weaves a subterranean world of pool halls so atmospheric you can smell the cigarettes. Paul Newman and Piper Laurie give incredible performances so twisted and nuanced with grief, guilt and longing it hurts.

Vertigo (1958)
Alfred Hitchcock creates a hypnotic sense of obsession and neurosis.

Blue Velvet (1986)
David Lynch's film takes a disturbing look at the underbelly of the American dream and uncovers a dark world.

Subway (1985)
Style over content some might say, but Luc Besson creates a magical world in the Paris metro. The fluorescent glow makes the surreal setting somehow plausible for Christopher Lambert's antics in this energetic thriller.

Lawrence of Arabia (1962)
David Lean's epic tale of the controversial British military figure.

Magnolia (1999)
Paul Thomas Anderson shows several slices of LA life. Cutting between stories does nothing to lose the tension that builds up to the climax, which sees it raining frogs and the ensemble cast burst into song. This takes place over the course of a life-changing 24 hours for all concerned.

Seven Samurai (1954)
Akira Kurosawa's classic about seven warriors who defend a town and defeat the baddies against the odds. *The Magnificent Seven* is the US remake.

SCRIPTWRITING

These films all have well-written screenplays, featuring tightly-structured narrative and three-dimensional characters that take the audience on an emotional journey.

Eternal Sunshine of the Spotless Mind (2004)
Charlie Kaufman creates an everyday reality mixed with surreal fantasy that is entertaining and thought-provoking.

Me and You and Everyone We Know (2005)
Miranda July deals with uncomfortable issues with wit and intelligence.

Almost Famous (2000)
Cameron Crowe creates wonderful characters that glisten.

American Beauty (1999)
Alan Ball draws interesting and believable characters without losing sight of the story.

Shakespeare In Love (1998)
Marc Norman and Tom Stoppard write with wit and intelligence, weaving Shakespearean references into the script with seeming ease.

Good Will Hunting (1997)
Matt Damon and Ben Affleck explore very human characters and realistic relationships with poignancy and emotion.

Pulp Fiction (1994)
Quentin Tarantino and Roger Avary's scriptwriting in this film is always worth looking at for innovative dialogue and structure.

The Piano (1993)
Evocative and enthralling, Jane Campion builds layer upon layer of story.

Chinatown (1974)
A tightly written and highly influential script in terms of style by Robert Towne.

Casablanca (1942)
Julius J Epstein, Philip G Epstein and Howard Koch provide a classic narrative.

PRODUCING

Here are some films that show how the production budget can influence the end product in unexpected ways.

The Avengers (1998)
Learn from this film in terms of not going into production until all of the pieces are in place.

Waterworld (1995)
In spite of a lavish budget this film failed to deliver at the box office.

Caravaggio (1986)
Made on a micro budget, this stylish British film created a stunning mise en scène through inventive use of composition and light.

The Blair Witch Project (1999)
Made on a micro budget, this film uses the low-budget home-made style as an asset. The home-video aesthetic adds to the immediacy and creates a sense of realism that works to intensify the horror.

The Full Monty (1997)
Made on a small budget profits soared when it became an unexpected box office hit.

The Lord of Rings Trilogy (2001/2002/2003)
The adaptation from book to screen was considered impossible to film for a long time.

PRODUCTION DESIGN

These films contain inspiring designs creating a visual language that helps to tell the story and develop the characters.

The Third Man (1949)
Joseph Bato provides an inventive use of the city of Vienna to help tell the story.

Closer (2004)
The designer, Tim Hatley, uses the geography of space to communicate what is going on between two couples whose lives entwine.

The Leopard (1963)
Set in 1860s Sicily, this exquisite film is a visual feast where Mario Garbuglia shows the death of the age of aristocracy.

2001: A Space Odyssey (1968)
Highly influential science-fiction film where Ronnie Bear paints a sterile future in white plastic.

Black Narcissus (1947)
Awe-inspiring painted backdrops by Alfred Junge take the audience to the Himalayan convent that is pulsing with vibrant energy.

Blade Runner (1982)
Lawrence G Paull designed this much copied dystopian vision where the architecture mixes past, present and possible future to disorientate.

Sleepy Hollow (1999)
Rick Heinrich's designs for the town and the woods combine the sweet and sour of classic fairytale imagery.

Caravaggio (1986)
Christopher Hobbs at his playful and anarchic best rips up the rule book on period design and gets closer to the spirit of the time.

Chinatown (1974)
This detective story is a classic in every way. Richard Sylbert uses a restricted colour palette to convey the dry parched 1930s LA during a water shortage.

Metropolis (1927)
Groundbreaking science-fiction film with stunning special effects and atmospheric set pieces by Otto Hunte.

Moulin Rouge! (2001)
Catherine Martin's designs are absolutely integral to Baz Luhrmann's films. This one goes completely hedonistic in a creative frenzy that fits with the raucous musical.

Essential viewing

CINEMATOGRAPHY

These examples show some of the stunning effects that can be achieved when camera and light are manipulated skillfully.

Citizen Kane (1941)
Famous for its deep-focus photography, courtesy of Gregg Toland.

Raging Bull (1980)
Michael Chapman's cinematography helps to take the audience into the ring and into the head of the protagonist.

Days of Heaven (1978)
Néstor Almendros creates a Texan-farm landscape that glistens like gold.

Crouching Tiger Hidden Dragon (2000)
Martial arts photography at its thrilling and dynamic best by Peter Pau.

Girl With A Pearl Earring (2003)
The painterly quality of camera and light created by Eduardo Serra captures each scene as if on canvas.

The Hustler (1961)
The skilled monochrome work by James Howe Wong creates impressive framing and lighting.

City of God (2002)
Rio de Janeiro in the 1960s is brought to life by César Charlone in rich saturated colours that make you feel the heat.

Wings of Desire (1987)
By filming the angels in blue-tinted monochrome and the humans in full colour, Henri Alekan skillfully juxtaposes the two perspectives to great effect.

Black Narcissus (1947)
Jack Cardiff's use of full-colour cinematography adds to the eroticism and energy of the film.

Rebecca (1940)
George Barnes creates stunning cinematography, where the house Manderlay is like another member of the cast possessed as it is by the former Mrs de Winter. Rebecca of the title is dead but lives on in the building.

SOUND

These films illustrates how sound can enhance the emotional energy within a film, and also provide a way of leading the audience to suspend its disbelief.

Raging Bull (1980)
Realistic sound effects, background noise and an effective score combined with periods of silence complement the on-screen action.

Reservoir Dogs (1992)
Tarantino's first feature made a big splash for inventive structure and style. The sound design is unusual and expressive; it's an energetic use of key sound effects and music.

Psycho (1960)
Unhinging sound effects and music combined with voices in characters' heads help create this hugely influential horror film.

The Godfather (1972)
This classic gangster film shows the mafia before the days of *The Sopranos*, with an evocative sound track.

The Red Shoes (1948)
Fairytale turns to obsession, jealousy and death.

Star Wars (1977)
The science fiction fantasy world is helped to life with memorable effects such as R2-D2, Chewbacca and light sabers.

Jaws (1975)
Provides high anxiety aided by the ominous musical score used whenever the shark is lurking.

Saving Private Ryan (1998)
This film pulls us into the horror of war through techniques that shock. The use of sound is integral to our feelings of terror and revulsion.

On The Waterfront (1954)
Gritty realism shot on-location in the docks gives this film an authentic documentary feel.

POST-PRODUCTION

These films convey a range of techniques used by the editor during post-production, which ultimately add to the drama, structure and pace of the finished film.

Battleship Potemkin (1925)
A classic example of montage editing; made in 1925, it still manages to be an exciting and emotional experience today.

Sunrise (1927)
Early use of flashbacks, dream-like fantasies and clever editing tricks make this 1927 silent masterpiece one to watch.

Citizen Kane (1941)
Effortless montage sequences to show the passing of time are among a multitude of clever editing tricks in this film.

Psycho (1960)
The shower scene is a great example of where a montage of shots makes you believe that you are seeing something more explicit than you actually are.

Straw Dogs (1971)
Relies on quick cuts and point of view shots to shock and cajole the audience. Intense and powerful film-making.

Jaws (1975)
Lots of parallel action and low-angle underwater shots from the shark's point of view combine to make gripping viewing.

Star Wars (1977)
Beautifully crafted, the original film is a perfectly paced fantasy that uses its vast array of long shots, mid-shots and close-ups to dazzling effect.

Dead Calm (1989)
Another perfectly paced film. A tense and claustrophobic thriller, it plays on parallel actions to create suspense and tension.

Die Hard (1988)
Fast-paced action movie that combines its widescreen cinematography with tight cutting, to force the audience's involvement in the action.

Moulin Rouge! (2001)
Those dazzling fast-cut dance montages – once seen, never forgotten!

PRODUCTION COURSES
UK / Europe / USA

www.aristotle.co.uk
Arista Development
Development skills workshops for UK/ Euro film/TV Professionals

www.filmeducation.org
Film Education
Development of film and media studies in schools and colleges

www.ft2.org.uk
FT2
Film and Television Freelance Training

www.globalfilmschool.com
Global Film School
Internet training and film school from NFTS (UK), UCLA (USA) and AFTR (Australia)

www.medialex-uk.com
Media Lex
Legal and Business training for film-makers

www.mediadesk.co.uk
MEDIA Plus programme
Information on European funding, production, festivals, markets, grants and training

www.nftsfilm-tv.ac.uk
NFTS
National Film and Television School

www.skillset.org
Skillset
The national training organisation for broadcast, film, video and multimedia

www.bfi.org.uk/education/study/skillset
Short Courses
Searchable database of BFI/ SkillSet supported film and media short courses

ORGANISATIONS
UK / Europe / USA

UK Film Institutes
www.bfi.org.uk
British Film Institute
National agency for encouraging and conserving the arts of film and television, Includes National Film and TV archive, Library, Sight & Sound magazine and support for film-makers

www.sgrin.co.uk
Sgrin
National film organisation for Wales

European Film Institutes
www.filminstitut.at
Austrian Film Institute

www.dfi.dk
Denmark Danish Film Institute

www.sea.fi
Finnish Film Archive

www.ses.fi
Finnish Film Foundation

www.bifi.fr
France
Bibliotheque du Film (BIFI)

www.cnc.fr
France
National Cinema Centre

www.filminstitute.de
German Film Institute

www.ffa.de
German Federal Film Board

www.centrum.is/filmfund
Iceland
Icelandic Film Fund

www.filmboard.ie
Ireland
Irish Film Board

www.cinetecamilano.it
Italy
Cineteca Italiana

www.nfi.no/nfi.htm
Norway
Norwegian Film Institute

FESTIVALS
UK / Europe / USA

UK Festivals
www.britfilms.com
Britfilms
Directories of British films and international film and video festivals

www.edfilmfest.org.uk
Edinburgh International Film Festival

www.geitf.co.uk
Guardian Edinburgh International Television Festival

www.kinofilm.org.uk
Kinofilm 2002 Manchester short film festival

www.latinamericanfilmfestival.com
Latin American Film Festival – London-based festival

www.leedsfilm.com
Leeds International Film Festival

www.lff.org.uk
London Film Festival

www.londonscreenings.com
London Screenings pre-MIFED buyers / sellers market and screenings info

www.raindancefilmfestival.org
Raindance Indie film festival and training

www.sidf.co.uk
Sheffield International Documentary Festival

www.rushes.co.uk/index.htm
Soho Shorts Rushes Shorts Film Festival

European Festivals
www.filmweb.no/biff
Bergen International Film Festival Norway

www.poff.ee
Black Nights Film Festival Estonia, special sections for children, student and animation

www.festival-cannes.org
Cannes Film Festival

www.mipcom.com
Cannes, MIPCOM

www.miptv.com
Cannes, MIPTV

www.filmfest.dk/dubrovnik
Dubrovnik Film and TV Festival Denmark

www.filmfestival.be
Flanders International Film Festiva. Belgium's most prominent festival in Ghent

www.kviff.com
Karlovy Vary Film Servis Festival
Czech film festival, Prague

www.filmfestivalrotterdam.com
Rotterdam International. Money prizes for first and second features, third world cinema, Cinemart and Exploding cinema.

www.labiennale.org/en/cinema
Venice Film Festival. World-renowned festival

www.wff.pl
Warsaw International Poland.
Key East European market

International Film Festivals
www.afifest.com
American Film Institute Festival

www.curtacinema.com.br
Brazil Festival do Rio – Rio de Janeiro Film Festival

www.hotdocs.ca
Hot Docs Canadian International Documentary Festival

www.jff.org.il
Jerusalem International Film Festival.
Prizes for Israeli cinema, human rights, Jewish themes and new directors.

www.melbournefilmfestival.com.au
Melbourne International Film Festival

www.ffm-montreal.org
Montreal Film Festival

www.sundance.org
Sundance Film Festival

www.sydfilm-fest.com.au
Sydney Film festival

www.bell.ca/filmfest
Toronto International Film Festival

www.viff.org
Vancouver International Film Festival
Expected audience of 14,000 see 300 films

FUNDING BODIES

www.artscouncil.org.uk
Arts Council of England
Suppport for film and video work by artists. For Lottery funding for film, see 'Film Council'

www.culture.gov.uk
DCMS
Department for Culture, Media and Sport. Responsible for government policy on film, relations with the film industry and government funding

www.filmcouncil.org.uk
Film Council
Information and application forms for Film Council / Lottery funding and information on all low-budget funding in the UK

www.arts.org.uk/londonarts
London Arts Board
Public sector funding and support for arts-related projects and businesses in London

www.mediadesk.co.uk
MEDIA Plus programme
Information on European funding, production, festivals, markets, grants and training

www.channel4.com
The Real Deal
Channel 4's Real Deal website

www.scottishscreen.com
Scottish Screen
National film organisation for Scotland
Urban East End Regeneration funding scheme

MINI INTERVIEWS

RAY BRADY
Director/Producer/Writer

How did you get into your job?
After messing around for two years with various Super 8 cameras I decided to pack in my job and do a foundation course followed by a degree in film and media.

What is the best bit about what you do?
When you make a film that works and you are then invited, all expenses paid, to major international film festivals, staying in five-star hotels and hanging out with the makers and stars of the other films in competition.

And the worst?
After completing a film, trying to find someone to sell it and commit a sensible P&A to promote and market it. Big films with big Hollywood stars have P&A budgets bigger than their actual production budgets. They get all the screens and interest from buyers and the press. Small indie films, unless they win major film awards, are completely ignored.

—

RYAN DRISCOLL
Film and Television Editor (post-production)

How did you get into your job?
I was lucky enough to be bought a Super 8 cine camera when I was 12 years old. I used to enjoy editing family holiday films. Then I got my friends to appear in dramas that I scripted and I would edit those. I sent them to the BBC and they won the 'Young Film-Maker of the Year' competition. From then I was hooked on editing.

What is the best bit about what you do?
Editing is like putting together jigsaw puzzles that have movement and sound. You spend all day long shifting the pieces around until they fit and you get paid for it!

And the worst?
Tight deadlines mean you are often under pressure to finish the job and because you are working with a director, a producer and other executives, the final cut is rarely yours.

PETER LAMONT
Production Designer

How did you get into your job?
I started at Pinewood Studios and worked my way up the art department.

What is the best bit about what you do?
The locations. It's wonderful to find a place that works for the script and in practical terms. You get to travel and see so many interesting places all over the world and have access you wouldn't have under normal circumstances.

And the worst?
Well if anything goes wrong (as the head of the art department) you're in the firing line and have to get it put right.

—

NICOLA LOWELL
Camera Assistant

How did you get into your job?
I started running and a friend gave me the telephone number of a camera woman. I called her and she got me to cable bash on a Saturday morning programme – it started properly from there!

What is the best bit about what you do?
Learning all the different elements of the camera and the job, and the randomness of each different job allows it to be varied and interesting. But mostly, building up my skills to get to the stage of operator one day.

And the worst?
It can be very hard physically and mentally at times depending on what job I'm on. But on the whole it's a great job and I love doing it.

ROBERTO NAPOLETANI
Location Manager

How did you get into your job?
Got some experience working on low-budget films. I sent out my CV to loads of location managers to see if they needed an assistant. I got a break and then one job led to another.

What is the best bit about what you do?
Scouting for the locations and meeting with lots of different people makes it varied and unpredictable. It's fantastic when you find a great place that works really well in the film.

And the worst?
Arranging parking for all of the vehicles on the shoot can get quite hairy. Obtaining filming permission from the council can be a frustrating experience.

—

NICK THOMAS
Location Sound Operator

How did you get into your job?
Pestered some production companies after university until one of them gave me some work experience. From there I asked the right questions and showed enthusiasm.

What is the best bit about what you do?
Travelling around and meeting different people; much better than being stuck in an office 9–5.

And the worst?
Standing in the pouring rain holding a boom mic for hour after hour.

—

MIKE TUCKER
Miniature Effects Supervisor

How did you get into your job?
I was a great fan of Dr Who, Blake's 7 and Ray Harryhausen films as a kid. I was also an avid model builder. When I realised that a job existed where I could actually combine these two obsessions I was hooked.

What is the best bit about what you do?
Getting back film rushes.

And the worst?
Paperwork! So much of it these days.

INDEX
Page numbers in **bold** denote illustrations

ACKNOWLEDGEMENTS AND CREDITS

I would like to thank everyone who has helped in the writing of this book, particularly the film-makers who have provided visual materials and valuable insight into film production.

Vital acknowledgments include my colleagues and students at London Metropolitan University, especially Charlotte Worthington and Lewis Jones for their support and encouragement. Lucy Tipton for her patience and guidance, Brian Morris, Renée Last and Sanaz Nazemi at AVA Publishing, and Kelvyn Laurence Smith for his design.

Thanks to all those who gave valuable contributions to the book – Ryan Driscoll, Karim Merie, Lily Elms, Nigel Kerr, Lucia Helenka, Campbell Graham, Darren Cathan, Greg Smith, Ray Brady, Des Brady, Hugo Wyhowski, Stuart Craig, Kave Quinn, Nicola Lowell, Mike Tucker, Peter Lamont, John Vanderpuije, Momoko Abe, Johannes Hausen, Kirstie Richardson, Joe Moran and Florence Peake.

And last but not least, heartfelt thanks go out to my family Alex, Mavis, Phil and Neil, all of my friends and Roberto.

—

CREDITS

Chapter 1 and pages 97 and 98:
Images courtesy of Karim Merie © Karim Merie www.kmphotos.com

Chapters 2 and 4:
Film stills from *Making a Killing* (2002) © Shining Light Productions. Distributed by Guerilla Films, available from amazon.co.uk

Chapter 5
Pages 109, 115 and 120, photographs courtesty of Hugo Wyhowski

⌃ 1 – 2: SOUND BOOTHS
Post-production sound is created in a controlled environment, such as in this sound-proof sound booth.

| – Exercise – |

Watch *Raging Bull* (1980) and make notes about the different sounds, where they appear and how they seem to be mixed to create different physical and emotional effects.